THE HUS BAND

Whisperer

KEVIN HINCKLEY

Author of
Habits, Hurts & Hangups

CFI
An Imprint of Cedar Fort, Inc.
Springville, Utah

ISBN 13: 978-1-4621-1384-2

Published by CFI, an imprint of Cedar Fort, Inc., 2373 W. 700 S., Springville, UT 84663
Distributed by Cedar Fort, Inc., www.cedarfort.com

LIBRARY OF CONGRESS CATALOGING-IN-PUBLICATION DATA

Hinckley, Kevin, author.
The husband whisperer / Kevin Hinckley.
  pages cm
Includes bibliographical references and index.
ISBN 978-1-4621-1384-2 (alk. paper)
1. Marriage--Religious aspects--Church of Jesus Christ of Latter-day Saints. 2. Communication--Religious aspects--Church of Jesus Christ of Latter-day Saints. I. Title.

BX8643.M36H56 2014
248.8'435--dc23

   2013049015

Cover design by Shawnda T. Craig
Cover design © 2014 Lyle Mortimer
Edited and typeset by Emily S. Chambers

Printed in the United States of America

10 9 8 7 6 5 4 3 2 1

Printed on acid-free paper

Dedicated to my mother, Eunice Hinckley,
an inspired whisperer, who taught me
how to find the real power in the still,
small voice; and to Cindy, who speaks
the language of the heart so well.

Other Titles by Kevin Hinckley:

Habits, Hurts & Hangups

Promptings or Me?

Burying Our Swords

Parenting the Strong-Willed Child

CONTENTS

INTRODUCTION

Circling the small enclosure, the young colt glances wildly out over the fence to the open field beyond. Impatiently, he stamps a foot and then impulsively bolts across to the other side of the pen, shaking his head with frustration. And fear.

The high railings around him seem to close in on all sides. Then he paws the soft dirt nervously. Usually, in the mornings, he has come to love running full speed across the meadow, just as the sun rises, and then returning at an easy gallop back to his mother's side—but only for a moment.

The sudden creak of a gate opening turns his head around. He is startled to see a man easing into the pen with him, a small length of rope dangling easily at his side. The colt trembles a bit and nervously moves to the farthest point away from this intruder. Shaking his head, he lets the man know he wants nothing to do with him—or the rope he carries.

Eyes rolling, the skittish young horse notes that the man does not immediately approach. Instead the man causally takes a seat on the ground, his back against the lower railing, and begins humming to himself and drawing in the dirt. The rope is placed on the ground beside him . . .

And the horse whispering has begun.

For centuries, spirited, strong-willed horses were captured in the wild and then "broken" so that they would be useful for man's purposes. The process of breaking—taming—was often a brutal contest of wills. This hard approach effectively domesticated the animal but risked losing the spirit of the horse.

In contrast, a number of trainers have found much more success with the well-documented "horse whispering" style of teaching. With this gentle and loving approach, trainers "whisper" to horses while treating them with dignity, consistency, and respect. Horse whispering, built on gentleness, draws heavily on the relationship between horse and trainer to calm and teach. It also helps preserve the spirit of the animal.

At this point, men reading this introduction are now thinking: *Wait! This is a book about husband whispering? Listen! I'm not some horse that needs to be trained or housebroken! And I'm not sure I even like being compared to a horse in the first place! In fact, I'm sure I'm not wild about my wife learning special "techniques" to manipulate me into doing what she wants me to do!*

Exactly!

In a book comparing the gentling of horses with communication in marriage, it becomes important to clarify what this book *is not*.

This is not a book about teaching wives magic words or language so that they win every argument. This is also not a book about learning the art of gentle manipulation. Nor is this a book about somehow domesticating men . . . Or finding ways to reward correct behavior with love and/or intimacy.

It is a book, for women, about learning to relate to men and using your divine nature to help us men to achieve all the Lord intends of us. Perhaps Neal A. Maxwell said it best when he noted, "we men know the women of God as wives, mothers, sisters, daughters, associates, and friends. *You seem to tame us and to gentle us, and yes, to teach us and to inspire us.* For you, we have admiration as well as affection, because righteousness is not a matter of role, nor goodness a matter of gender.[1]

Horse whisperers learned long ago that the true strength of these powerful animals could be seriously compromised in a harsh effort to simply change them. They came to know what the Lord has always known: each of us responds and grows by learning to follow the still, small voice. The Spirit does not shout nor force. Its truths come wrapped in gentleness and love.

Conversely, all of us tend to avoid and recoil at anger and attacks with a variety of negative responses—none of them helpful!

What is husband whispering then? It is the process of being led by the Lady Wisdom within (see chapter three!) to bring increased understanding and beauty to your marriage. It is learning to communicate from the deepest, most honest part of you. And doing it in such way that it draws out the same honesty in him.

For this reason, husband whispering—much like horse whispering—is as much about how the husband whisperer acts, what she says, and who she is, than of trying to change the husband. As she grows and nurtures, changes will come. He will respond to your gentling touch and approach.

The good news is that it is doubtful you'll ever have to sit in a dusty corral, playing in the dirt—unless, of course, you really like corrals and dirt!

The only thing bridled may be the words you say and the wonderful whispering way in which you say them.

Notes

1 Neal A. Maxwell, "The Women of God," *Ensign*, May 1978; emphasis added.

1

HEAVEN IS WHISPERING

Rachel shouts more than she wished she did. She knows it. Her husband and kids know it. The neighbors three blocks over know it.

And she hates it.

Growing up the youngest with four brothers, Rachel's home was always a swirl of activity and competition. Arguments were frequent. She learned early that often the loudest voice was the one to be heard.

However, with her own family now, there is nothing she hates more than to hear her own teenage children arguing and yelling. She cringes when she hears them but then feels like she needs to be the loudest to be heard—again.

Rachel also knows how she feels after she and her husband, Lee, have been arguing. As with her kids, she will find her voice louder than she intends, especially when she feels like Lee is not listening to her. Yet she is also coming to see that the more she yells, the more Lee seems to be tuning her out. And without her yelling, he simply doesn't pay attention to what she tries to say. That leaves her even more frustrated—but also feeling guilty about the times she yells. It seems like such an endless cycle!

Sound familiar? It's never a great parenting moment when you are yelling at the kids—about their yelling! Or being stuck in the pattern of having no one listen to you until you do yell before they take you seriously.

If this sounds familiar, reading a book about the virtues of talking more gently might sound like a prescription for being ignored all together.

Obviously, you've never been married to a husband who has totally bonded with his computer screen. If I were to talk softer, I'd become the invisible woman, wandering around the house like a disembodied spirit! I don't need to whisper. I need a bullhorn and a taser!

And I know it can often feel that way. Yet the louder and louder cycle never seems to work in the long run, leaving only frustrated wives and deaf children . . .

In *The Screwtape Letters*, C. S. Lewis's devil detests music and silence. Hell, he crowed, was filled with furious noise: "The audible expression of all that is exultant, ruthless and virile. . . . We will make the whole universe a noise. . . . We have already made great strides in this direction as regards the Earth. The melodies and silences of Heaven will be shouted down in the end."

The eternal reality is this: heaven whispers and revels in still-ness! (Okay, there was the "shouting for joy" moment, but that was a pretty exciting moment.) The Prophet Joseph Smith described the revelatory spirit as "the still small voice, which *whispereth* through and pierceth all things." His own reaction to that penetrating yet powerful voice was that "often times it maketh my bones to quake" (D&C 85:6). What an interesting reaction to a whisper!

Heaven's Whispers

Heaven, it would seem, prefers to speak in quieter tones, communicating vital eternal wisdom with a measured voice. As we will discover, heavenly whisperings are the Lord's divine pattern—His loving voice to mankind. It is the pattern by which we are to speak to one another if we want to be like him.

Personally, I might wish many times that the Spirit spoke with a louder voice. If I'm about to engage in a stupid activity, it would seem like a louder warning from above might help get my attention. But He doesn't do that. We do get spiritual warnings before we do things we shouldn't but not with a celestial bullhorn. Instead, as we know, we receive quiet nudges of our conscience, a discomforting stirring of a concerned conscious.

Why is the Spirit so quiet? Why wouldn't it give louder and more insistent warnings? Wouldn't that keep you on a straighter path? It seems like there would be a lot less sinning if alarms went off in your head prior to a potential sin!

Keep in mind that we are fallen mortals living a veiled experience. This world, with all its distractions, is not your home. During this journey, it is essential to have an ongoing dialogue with an infinite, eternal heaven-home. The reality is that what little you can feel and hear from above is severely hampered by the static of earthbound hearts and ears.

To paraphrase Moroni, "And thou hast made us that we could [understand] but little, because of the [mortalness] of our [brains]" (Ether 12:23). You are simply trapped inside a fallen mind that struggles to comprehend the vastness of God's plan for you.

But while your human frailties struggle to understand, your body is the imperfect mortal coil that surrounds the real you—your premortal, well-schooled spirit. For a spirit that spent thousands of years in the presence of Heavenly Father, this earth experience must be incredibly frustrating. If anyone deserves to scream, it is your spirit!

(*You're going to do what? Again? Please no!*)

Our ability to understand heaven is further hamstrung by life's experiences that shape us and can help us form false perceptions of ourselves. It is much like Albert Einstein trying to explain the laws of physics to a hungry two-year-old. In truth, your mortality is so poorly equipped to comprehend heaven that it is a tender mercy that you succeed as often as you do.

Yet despite the gap between heaven and earth, your spirit is perfectly tuned to hear and understand. How is this done? Through the medium of the Spirit. The Holy Ghost translates, making "intercession with groaning that cannot be expressed" (see Romans 8:26). It speaks a language out of the range of mortal ears. The still, small voice is that bridging language.

I recently sat in the temple with a young couple soon to be married. During the session, I watched as he turned and looked at her. Feeling his gaze she looked over at him. Both smiled. Then, with a tenderness born of great love, they communicated briefly without a word being spoken. It was a reminder to me that the most powerful of all communications uses very few words. Looks, feelings, and facial expressions all share a much deeper and powerful level of "conversation" beyond what we are aware.

The quiet whispering voice of the Spirit is merely the outer edge of celestial-like outflow of the Lord's communication with us. Any words heard are the smallest portion of what is being sent. To receive what is intended, you quiet worldly intrusions. You limit the intrusions and opinions of your own brain—and you listen with your heart.

Heaven may whisper, but your spirit is eagerly attuned to hear its shoutings!

The World's Voice

Elder Marvin K. Ashton pointed out, "Too often we are inclined to be impressed with the loud, noisy, and dramatic. Students and members in general are sometimes led away from the paths of success because they are swayed by the sensational and artificial light. Very often in today's busy world we ignore the quiet promptings of our leaders and those who guide with soft words."[1]

Again, at times, you might wish His voice was louder and clearer. When He says that He stands at your door and knocks (Revelation 3:20), you often don't hear it because of the volume of noise in your own house. How often has His gentle knocking been overlooked by the mindless and the mundane!

Recently I was filling up my car with gas. As I did so, two teens pulled up to the next adjacent pump. As they did, they rolled down their windows and turned up the music in their car. The loud thumping of their oversize speakers drowned out any chance of any conversation for the next ten square blocks around them. As you might have guessed, the boys were not listening to Vivaldi or Beethoven. The music was not just loud, it was also angry and vile.

As I drove away, I could picture these music aficionados trying to go to sleep with earphones jammed in their ears so that they never had to be separated from the constant beat of a driving, angry bass in their ears. Their painful alternative? They might have to listen to one another or their parents or even silence. So depressing! In that atmosphere, I could easily see how the still, small voice would have virtually no opportunity to impact their lives—at least while the music was on.

The sound of modern earth life is loud, crass, and competitive. Many current sporting events are filled with "trash talking" and angry taunts. Popular movies, TV shows, video games, pop music, and fashion celebrate coarseness in the name of being "edgy." And the common denominators are angry, loud voices, drowning out everything else around them.

Political commentary has evolved the same way. In the interest of hearing all sides, loud debate is encouraged by "moderators." However, opposing sides are not there to listen, only to noisily control the discussion. To win the debate you must be heard—in the loudest voice possible! Most news producers decided long ago that compromise and agreement do not make for compelling TV.

How fascinating, then, that the Lord chose to communicate vital, eternal, healing, saving, exalting knowledge in such quiet tones. In our most sacred of all places, the temple, we are encouraged to communicate with one another in whispers so that we might feel the quiet reverence of the Spirit. It is meant to be a place separate from the world physically but also separated from the world spiritually. To do that, the harsh sounds of the world must be screened out that heaven may speak to hearts straining to listen.

In your daily living, the art of learning to communicate with "perfect mildness" (Helaman 5:30) may not come so easily. As Rachel discovered, she had learned early in life that she would need to be loud in order to be heard. Her current life is busy and chaotic. Evenings are a swirl of homework and practices and activities. It becomes easy for family's voices to rise in order to compete with each other. The loudest voice wins . . . and everyone else loses.

Whispers

Learning to *hear whisperings* is critical to *being a whisperer*. It is learning to recognize the language you wish to speak. If you are to become like Him, you first must learn to speak like He does.

At the risk of giving away too many trade secrets, I learned early in my counseling some natural techniques for making sure my clients remembered important points of our discussion. While many things might be said in the course of a regular counseling session, some points are obviously more critical. Finding a way to emphasize these points, in the mind of the client, becomes key.

In working with an overprotective mom, for instance, I tried to help her see the negative effects her constant micromanaging was having in the life of her fifteen-year-old son. She was full of constant fear and worry and angst about the quality of his school work. The more he balked at the demands of school, the more she tried to control every aspect of his life. In her mind, it was the only way she knew to make sure he did everything she felt he needed to do.

Finally, after listening to her express her fears, I quietly leaned forward and whispered softly to her, "My dear, you might need to let him fail this class. It could be the only way he's going to learn. If you keep doing everything for him, he will still be living with you when he's thirty and doing nothing but playing video games all night long!"

She grimaced and whispered back, "I love him but I don't want him still living with us at thirty!"

As we will discuss later, the combination of 1) increased eye contact, 2) closeness, and 3) and a more whispered voice communicated to her an important point she needed to hear. She noted the sudden change in my tone and immediately responded with a softer voice as well. This is because we have a natural human tendency to match or mirror one another. I softened and so did she. She even leaned more forward than I did.

In much the same way, straining to understand heaven's softer voice causes you to pay closer attention. As you strive more diligently to hear its gentle counsel, you learn and remember. And you are then more likely to copy its milder approach in your conversations with others.

The difficult question you need to ask yourself is: How well do you listen and respond to critical whisperings from heaven? Do you recognize when you're being whispered to, or do you tend to wait for a more dramatic answer? Do you miss the quieter communications that might have been there all along?

Oliver Cowdery felt impressed that he should be helping Joseph Smith translate the Book of Mormon while he was still lodging with the prophet's family in Palmyra. Through prayer, he sought for guidance to know what to do. The Lord answered his askings with an outpouring of the Spirit. Acting on those promptings, Oliver then traveled to Harmony, Pennsylvania, to meet with the prophet and begin the work of translation.

It is interesting to note that despite the fact that Oliver had been given answers, he was still filled with doubts. He questioned whether what he had felt had actually been a prompting to help in the translation process. For this reason, he sought a revelation from Joseph to know if he'd actually had a revelation.

"Behold," the Lord responded, "as often as thou hast inquired thou hast received instruction of my Spirit" (D&C 6:14). *Oliver, though you may not have known it, I've answered your prayers as often as you've asked.* "If it had not been so, thou wouldst not have come to [Harmony] where thou art at this time" (ibid.). *You are here, aren't you?*

And then the Lord's explanation. "Behold, thou knowest that thou hast inquired of me and I did enlighten thy mind; and now I tell thee these things that thou mayest know that thou hast been enlightened by the Spirit of truth" (D&C 6:15).

Without education and spiritual maturity, it is possible to have been influenced by the still, small voice—even followed it—and not known it. Because the Spirit is so quiet and often so subtle, it takes effort and experience to hear it and recognize it. You have to clear away distractions so that you "make place" (Alma 32:21) for the seed of knowledge to be planted. Otherwise it can be quickly cast out by the competing and louder sounds of the world. Perhaps, at that moment, the unbelief you might experience is simply a lack of trust in your own abilities to hear it.

Recently, I talked with a teenage girl who doubted if she had a testimony of the Church. Because of those doubts she wavered on whether to stay with the Church or to leave it. She had lived an obedient life and her parents were both loving and active. She spoke to me because she knew her struggles would be devastating to her parents.

"Can I ask you some questions?" I asked.

She nodded silently.

"Have you ever prayed and gotten an answer to prayer?" I asked.

"Yes," she responded quickly.

"What happened?"

"I prayed that I'd do good on a test."

"And?"

"And I did!" she said.

"So the way you know you received an answer was that the thing you prayed for happened?"

She nodded again.

"That is certainly one way," I agreed. "But have you ever asked something in prayer and felt the Spirit give you an answer?"

"To be honest, I'm really not sure."

Her response was typical of many youth in the Church. Like our Christian brothers and sisters in other faiths, the belief in prayer is that 1) If I ask for something and the thing happens, the answer must be yes. 2) If I ask for something and it doesn't happen, God must have said no. For them, answers to prayers are simply things that can be seen. It happened or it didn't. What they miss is learning how often the answer to a prayer might be simple information or nudging to do something.

I could immediately see why she wasn't sure about her testimony. She didn't know what to listen for.

I then asked, "Have you ever gone to a really good testimony meeting?"

Her eyes brightened. "Yeah, there was a really good one at EFY! It was amazing!"

"Great!" I said. "Did you feel the Spirit?"

"Yeah! It was really cool!"

"What was the Spirit saying to you in that testimony meeting?"

Well, that stopped her. She had felt the Spirit, heard the voice, but never considered what feeling the Spirit *meant*!

We then had a discussion that the Spirit she felt was real and powerful. And that it was bearing witness—to her—that what was being said in the testimony meeting was true. Things like: Joseph

Smith was a prophet. The Book of Mormon is true. This is the church of Jesus Christ.

In other words, at EFY she had a received a spiritual confirmation about the truthfulness of the Church but didn't know it. The Spirit had borne witness to her many times and she hadn't known exactly what it meant. She only knew that it felt good!

Finally, we talked about how she could use those EFY testimony feelings as a pattern at other times in her life. I told her that when she did, she'd ultimately be surprised that the Holy Ghost was talking to her far more often than she knew. It was there on a regular basis, yet she'd been looking for something else as a confirmation.

In conclusion, the more you recognize the heavenly pattern of communication, the easier it is for you to duplicate that pattern in your daily communications with those around you. You are trying to emulate a quiet voice that "pierces" to the core. It is a voice that is mild but full of power and strength.

At the moment, that could sound like a miracle. And, at first, it might just be. There will certainly be some trial and error, as well as some learning on the part of your husband and children. But I promise they can learn!

It is certainly that softer voice the Prophet Elijah heard and responded to. As he stood upon a mountain, the scripture tells us that the Lord *passed by*. "And, behold, the Lord passed by, and a great and strong wind rent the mountains." You have probably been in situations and conversations that felt more like a great and strong wind. When that happens, you either duck to protect yourself or you flee the storm. Either way you don't want to stand there exposed during someone's verbal hurricane.

"But the Lord was not in the wind." For the righteous trying to do the right thing, the Lord is not in the storms that rent the mountains around you. He is not in the trials that buffet you. It is not how He works.

"And after the wind an earthquake . . . and after the earthquake a fire . . ." Despite all the more dramatic things around Elijah, "the Lord was not. . . ." He simply was not. Where he was was in "a still small voice" (1 Kings 19:11–12).

It is this voice that asks: "What doest thou here, Elijah?"

If you are to going to learn to speak with powerful whisperings, you will first need to learn to hear powerful whisperings from above. As you listen and learn, you can emulate the style and approach the Lord takes with you. As you do so, you are well on your way to being a peaceable whisperer.

Notes

1 "A Still Voice of Perfect Mildness," BYU Speeches, 20 February, 1990.

2
SELF-WHISPERING

The art of whispering begins with you. It begins with how you see yourself and how you speak to yourself. Those internal conversations, harsh or gentle, say a lot about you. It suggests just what opinion you have of yourself and your own internal self-image. As we will discover, it can be pretty difficult to husband whisper when your own inside conversation is critical and demeaning.

When she was young, Shelly grew up afraid of her dad. He worked long hours at a job he hated. He often came home angry and frustrated with events at work—and that anger often spilled out onto Shelly and her two brothers and their mother. His tone was often critical and could be cutting and demeaning. Everyone in her family lived a tense, uneasy life at those times when Dad was home. *Will this make Dad mad?* was the first consideration of any family decision.

When Shelly married Chad, she soon realized that he too was prone to angry outbursts. But she had decided, after a lifetime of watching her passive and bullied mother, that she would be different. If Chad was angry, she would not let him get away with it. But as a result, their arguments could be pointed and quite attacking at times. Afterward, Shelly would find herself prone to painful migraines and bouts of depression. She also would become upset when she would hear her kids fighting. Her response was to dish out immediate punishments when she would hear them do it.

It is impossible for us to come to any relationship without a history. Each of us are the sum total of all the relationships and interactions we've ever had—probably stretching into the premortal life! Each social association we've had plays a role in developing how we see other people, how much or little we trust, how safe we feel around others, and who we choose to spend our time with.

For instance, your childhood was a laboratory of people training and communication. The adults around you taught you how to interact and respond to other people. At your youngest ages, you watched as adults and family members were affectionate, had conflicts, and dealt with disappointment and success. You saw the result of their choices. Thus, it would not have been unusual for you to say to yourself, "When I'm a mom, I'll do _____."

Children learn quickly which adults seem to get what they want and how they got it. One woman described her experience of watching her mother use illness as a way of avoiding situations and people. "She would tell us kids she wasn't feeling well when there was something she didn't want to do. But I watched her. We knew she just didn't want to do things."

Children quickly learn the effective value of using anger to get what they want. They watch as adults escalate disagreements louder and louder. They learn whether the adults got what they wanted when they shouted or not. Did the noisiest and most persistent usually get their way? Also, what were the consequences of getting really angry? Was it rewarded or punished?

In the end, you do what works. You repeat behavior that results in getting what you want—and you stop behavior that doesn't.

Unfortunately, if anger or yelling has produced what you wanted in life, you will tend to keep using it, even though you might feel guilty that you did. The good news is that whispering also works. But you might have to experience success in order to believe it.

Self-Image

In addition, every relationship, past and present, plays a role in creating your internal self-image. Your image is that inside photograph you carry in your mind of just how you see yourself. This mental snapshot is a quick view of how *you assume* others see you as well. Living in society is like walking around in a house of mirrors. You see yourself in others—in how they respond to you and how you respond to them.

Are you largely invisible? Are people generally glad to see you? Do you believe you're seen as an equal or are you a bit insecure that maybe you are just not as smart or talented as everyone else. When someone is critical toward you, do you take it personally or just consider the source? Your internal self-image takes all this into consideration, and it plays a major role in the daily decisions you make.

When I ask clients about their self-image, they almost always tend to look away. The reality is that internal view, unvarnished and real, can be pretty negative and painful. When I ask them to describe what they *really* see, I start hearing labels such as loser, dumb, or fat.

So, just how do you see you? Take moment and close your eyes. If there was an old childhood photograph from when you were younger, one that correctly reveals the "real you," what would it show? How old are you in the picture? What are you doing? Can you see the look on your face? Are you alone or with someone? What would be the reaction of someone looking at you? What feelings well up inside you as you look at it? Are you remembering an actual photograph or your version of it?

Okay, you can stop now! I know how fun that can be—or not! These pictures can be very uncomfortable, but they can give you an idea of just what you think of yourself. Your initial reaction to that picture is probably the most accurate.

It is this internal view that determined so many of the choices you've made in your life. It guided the friends you chose and what job you trained and applied for. It played a role in who you dated and who you married. And it continues to shape how you relate to people around you. It even guides how much you are willing to risk and how you deal with conflict.

For Shelly, years of critical comments left her wary of any interactions. Hearing angry voices caused an immediate reaction. Her stomach would churn and her heart would start pounding. Yet she also wanted to make sure she wouldn't be submissive like her mother. Therefore, she would become angry if yelled at and respond with her own anger. But she would then be depressed for days afterward because she had been the one being loudest and angriest!

First, Whisper Thyself!

In truth, you cannot gentle the soul of another while a storm rages within yourself. "Peace, be still" must begin first in your own heart before it can spread outward. Each of us struggles with our own earth-stains, those private wounds and scars mortality gives us from time to time. Living in a telestial setting exposes you to a constant flow of imperfection and evil, thoughtlessness and malice, pride and blunder. Each non-celestial interaction is an affront to your spiritual soul and a constant reminder of the harshness you now live in. At some level, your spirit must recoil at how far you are from the peace of your former heavenly home.

For this reason, if you are going to gentle others, you begin by allowing your own gentling; the whisperer must first be whispered to. You commence by tuning your spiritual ears to hear softer and more powerful messages.

The Apostle Paul gives us a beautiful blueprint for whispering. In his wonderful letter to the saints in Corinth, he tries to have them become more unified. "The eye cannot say unto the hand," he explains, "I have no need of thee; nor again the head to the feet, I have no need of you" (1 Corinthians 12:21). In other words, members of the fledgling branch of the Church needed to see themselves as equals, regardless of their life experiences.

This was especially true of those who saw themselves as "more feeble" or "less comely"; those who had come to believe they were the "least of the saints" (D&C 89). Paul teaches that these are the walking wounded among us. But he would also have us understand that the Lord has blessed the feeble with compensating gifts. He teaches that they have received a "more abundant honour" (1 Corinthians 12:24) from God and often are in possession of a "best gift," a "more excellent way" (1 Corinthians 12:31).

For those of us conscious of our own feebleness, we plead, *Lord! Please show me this more excellent way because so often I only see the feeble and less comely in myself. . . .*

Paul's stirring response comes in the first verse of the next chapter. "Though I speak with the tongues of men and of angels," he warns, "and have not charity . . . I am nothing" (1 Corinthians 13:1, 2). *But*, we might protest, *how can I be charitable when I am most conscious of my own faults?*

If we're not careful, we might miss the beautiful lesson Paul is teaching us. "For we know in part, and we prophesy in part" (1 Corinthians 13:9). *Some things we know and some things we don't yet know.* For instance, he explains, "When I was a child, I spake as a child, I understood as a child, I thought as a child: but when I become a man, I put away childish things" (1 Corinthians 13:11).

When I was younger—physically/spiritually/intellectually—my understanding was so limited. I saw things from a narrow perspective and didn't understand what was true and what was not. I believed things about myself that were not true. But I wasn't old enough or experienced enough to filter out the lies from the truth.

Paul goes on. "For now we see through a glass, darkly." *In the present, trying to see the real me is like looking into a mirror in the darkness. I can only see a vague outline of myself. I can't see past the defining messages I heard when I was a child.* "Now I know in part . . ." *For the present, I only know what a child would know.* ". . . but then shall I know even as also I am known." *Someday in the future, I will know me as I am known by the Lord. I will finally see me as God sees me. And I will finally believe His unfiltered vision of who I am in His eyes.*

Paul then concludes, "And now abideth faith, hope, charity, these three; but the greatest of these is charity" (1 Corinthians 13:13). Charity for who? True, this is charity for all people. But in this instance?

Charity for me. Faith and hope that I can actually gain a true vision of the real me.

If you would whisper peace to others, you begin by first offering charity and mercy to yourself. You come to recognize that a darkened view of yourself shows you little of who you really are. For this reason, you have too often relied on the imperfect opinion of others. Elder Enzio Busche, an emeritus member of the Quorum of the Seventy, describes a woman he knew in Germany who was one of the "less comely" members of his ward.

> Shortly after our baptism, Jutta and I became aware of an elderly sister named Sister Maischt, whose enthusiasm for the gospel and the Church was so extraordinary that the shabbiness of her outward appearance did not matter much.
>
> From her looks, she was as close to a fairy tale witch as anyone I have ever seen—always wearing the same, long, ugly black dress and never clean, always smelly. She simply did not try to look groomed or acceptable . . .
>
> She lived in a shed without plumbing or electricity and lived off the food she grew on her land. She never talked about the details.
>
> When anyone asked her about her background, she would immediately change the subject and talk about the goodness of Christ, the support of angels, and her testimony of the Book of Mormon . . .
>
> One day, my wife and I discussed Sister Maischt and the fact that she walked two hours one way to go to church. We debated whether we should make the sacrifice and leave thirty minutes earlier on Sundays to give her a ride. We felt good as finally agreed to do this service for her.
>
> How surprised I was, however, when I presented her with our suggestion. She said: "Brother Busche, you cannot do this to me. I'm an old lady. How can I ever show the Lord how much I love Him, how much I adore Him, how much I depend on His atoning sacrifice for my salvation and my desire to serve Him?
>
> "I'm too old and too ugly and too forgetful to serve as the

Relief Society president or even a teacher. The greatest joy of my life is on Sunday when I can get up early in the morning, walk to church, and take the sacrament. Yes it is a long walk and, yes, my legs hurt and my back hurts, but every step I rejoice.

"As I walk I sing the hymns . . . because my walk is a celebration of my Savior and Lord, Jesus Christ. And you want to take this away from me? You can't do this to me. Let me walk."[1]

So often, we gaze on only the outward appearance and see only what the rest of the world sees. You may even do that with yourself. Even the prophet Moroni peered down the corridors of time and saw the mixed reaction that would greet the publishing of the Book of Mormon. Worried that his writing weaknesses might hamper future readers, he notes, "And it came to pass that I prayed unto the Lord that he would give unto the Gentiles grace, that they might have charity" (Ether 12:36). In other words, he knew that if the future gentiles would receive the gift of grace, it would then fill them with love and charity and then they'd be more open to the message of book.

In like manner, if you are willing to accept the Lord's gift of grace, you will be filled with the softening and ennobling power of charity—not just for others, but also for yourself. Grace is the key that unlocks your ability to be changed by his love. It is how we receive "the mighty change," receiving "his image in [our] countenances" (Alma 5:14).

More important, the gift of grace whispers that His view of you is more accurate than any false images you might carry about yourself. The Holy Ghost can then confirm this to your heart and help change the faulty self-image you carry.

The Voice of Peace

Self-whispering is the process of being continually fed spiritual truths through the same gift of the Holy Ghost. It teaches truth and brings us grace. It reaffirms who we really are and the love Heavenly Father has for us. It whispers to us that we need not be perfect to be loved and that the Atonement will transform us into his image (Alma 5). As we will discuss in chapter ten, when you stop and listen, eternal truths can "distill" upon you as "the dews from heaven" (D&C 121:45) and you will know "the truth of all things" (Moroni 10:5). These truths help you reject lies as the Spirit bears witness to what is real and what is not.

When you listen to those gentle whisperings, you are reminded of eternal truths about yourself and about your Heavenly Father:

I know you, and I've always known you.

My voice is quiet and still.

My path and plan for you will bring you greater peace than your plans for you.

You don't have to be perfect to be loved.

There are those around you who love you.

This voice brings hope and calms the natural fears and anxiety you might have about life's decisions and about others. It is the same voice that calmed the storms, but you must first "stop and stand still" in order to hear it.

On the other hand, when you fail to listen to the Spirit's quiet whisperings, other voices can crowd in on you. You are then more vulnerable to believe any negative voices that sought to define you as you grew. These critical voices can cloud and confuse. They sow doubt and confusion. You can then overreact to negative comments—right or wrong—of others. Filled with these distortions, your insecurities and doubts can run like a river of anxiety just below the surface. Taking council from those fears causes you to more quickly agree with those negative comments and believe them as truths.

Michelle is amazing. At any ward function she can be found cooking or organizing. The bishopric knows that she can be called to any calling and that it will get done. Michelle's husband, Rick, is elder's quorum president and a successful accountant. Other women look at Michelle with a mixture of envy and wonder. *How does she do it?*

In reality, Michelle knows little peace. Though she reads her scriptures daily, she rarely finds peace. Instead, she is reminded of everything she fears she's not doing. Her weaknesses shout at her. If her family sits back to watch a movie, she is unable to join them for more than a few minutes before she needs to be up and doing—something.

Whenever any compliments are extended, she becomes uncomfortable and quickly changes the subject. When asked to give a talk in church, Michelle will spend weeks writing and rewriting it. And she will never be happy with the final product. Nor does she believe any positive feedback from others.

They're just saying that to be nice, she thinks.

Growing up, Michelle was the third of five daughters. Her oldest sister went to medical school. The next oldest is musically talented and went to college on a music scholarship. Michelle was the "good girl." She was always trying to do the right thing. Young women leaders praised her and her teachers adored her.

But Michelle's grades and achievements never quite matched

the accomplishments of her two older sisters. She always quietly lived in their shadows and watched their praises. She watched them both succeed and has always felt like she could never match them.

Michelle's unending self-critique spills over onto her kids and her husband. Because she is always reminding them to clean their rooms or their appearance, they complain that they can never do anything right. In reality, her constant pickiness is simply part of her never feeling like she is a good enough mother or housekeeper.

Warning! The art of husband whispering is *not* the art of gently teaching husband and family to become more obsessive compulsive or perfectionists! It is the art of learning to walk the "peaceable walk with the children of men" (Moroni 7:4). Helping set a more peaceful tone around us first involves finding peace in our own souls.

For Michelle, self-whispering involves learning to see herself more like God sees her. It involves surrendering her will to the Lord and letting Him whisper to her and slowly change her. The classic quote from C. S. Lewis says it best:

> Imagine yourself as a living house. God comes in to rebuild that house. At first, perhaps, you can understand what He is doing. He is getting the drains right and stopping the leaks in the roof and so on: you knew that those jobs needed doing and so you are not surprised.
>
> But presently He starts knocking the house about in a way that hurts abominably and does not seem to make sense. What on earth is He up to?
>
> The explanation is that He is building quite a different house from the one you thought of—throwing out a new wing here, putting on an extra floor there, running up towers, making courtyards.

You thought you were going to be made into a decent little cottage: but He is building a palace.[2]

Whispering, in the end, becomes much more natural as you see the you God sees. Filled with His love, you treat yourself more kindly. You are less self judgmental—because He is! As your self-image spiritually matures, speaking to others around you becomes the easy next step. Filled with love, you extend love. Granted mercy, you extend mercy. Seen in a new light, you spot the light in those around you. Whispered to, and you, in turn, whisper.

Notes

1 F. Enzio Busche, *Yearning for the Living God* (Salt Lake City: Deseret Book, 2004), 166.
2 C. S. Lewis, *Mere Christianity* (New York: HarperCollins, 2001), 176.

3
DIVINE NATURE AND LADY WISDOM

Help me be me,
As you see me!
—AA Prayer

In the last chapter, we talked about allowing yourself to be whispered to so you can change any negative self-images that block your ability to allow heaven's whispers to flow through you. For many women, changing that image means gaining a clearer understanding of what a newer image might be. It means understanding the beautiful healing power contained in your eternal divine nature.

Jennifer awoke feeling restless. The kids had all left for school, and she had a long list of things she needed to get done. As she started to sort laundry, the feelings of unease got progressively worse. Finally, she recognized the feelings as a prompting to do something.

But what?

As she prayerfully searched her mind, she was immediately filled with thoughts of a young mother in the ward who struggled with depression. This mother had three small kids and a husband who worked long hours. Immediately Jennifer knew what she needed to do.

Setting aside her long list of things to do, she grabbed her keys and drove over to the home of the young mother. When the harried mom opened the door, Jennifer grinned and explained she was there to watch the kids for the morning while she got away for a few hours. Tears came to her tired eyes, and an exhausted mom gratefully left for a much-needed break.

Later in the day, Jennifer quietly returned home, immediately went back to work, and didn't mention her actions to her family or anyone else. Outward recognition was not her motivation. Her loving act came to light only when the grateful mother reported it to me.

Jennifer's willingness to follow her promptings was followed by sweet selfless service. She had listened and responded to an unspoken request. And, more remarkably, for a woman in the kingdom of God, her prompt action and loving ministering was not that unusual.

Millions of churches meet every Sabbath day. In some places the churches are packed. In others, many pews remain empty. However, one common theme exists in all these settings, regardless of the denomination: more women will be in attendance than men.

Statistics confirm what we see each Sunday:

> The typical US congregation draws a crowd that's 61 percent female, 39 percent male. Internationally, up to nine women attend church for every one man.
>
> On any given Sunday, there are ten million more adult women than men at church.

Twenty-five percent of married, active women will go to church without their husbands.[1]

Churches bleed men—and in large numbers. And while these numbers are distressing to any religious group trying to recapture the men of their congregations, they do remind us of one important fact: in general, women are generally more spiritually inclined than are men.

Elder Neal A. Maxwell noted, "In our modern kingdom, it is no accident that women were, through the Relief Society, assigned compassionate service. *So often the service of women seems instinctive, while that of some men seems more labored.*"[2]

At the crucifixion of the Savior, Matthew notes that "many women were there beholding afar off" (Matthew 27:55). In fact, at many points in the Savior's life, faithful women appeared as examples and role models of faith and belief. In spiritual activities, discussions, service projects, and so on, there were always many more women beholding!

This pattern may hold true even in the spirit world. Joseph F. Smith was blessed to see and record the visit of the Savior to the spirit world following His crucifixion. President Smith described a vast congregation of the righteous waiting for their resurrection. The Savior organized the "great and mighty ones" into a celestial missionary force to bring the gospel to those "in darkness" and "in bondage" in the world of spirits.

In listing these great ones preparing to bring light to those in darkness, President Smith made particular note of one group organized and ready for this massive mission of salvation: "And our glorious Mother Eve, with many of her faithful daughters who had lived through the ages and worshiped the true and living God"

(D&C 138:39). This missionary force is powerful and notable alongside patriarchs such as Adam, Abel, and Noah.

In the scriptures, the list of women's names is relatively small. Their contribution, on the other hand, was pivotal. Whether it be the widow's mite or Mary's visit with the risen Lord, their input has been crucial to history.

Again, Neal Maxwell observes,

> When the real history of mankind is fully disclosed, will it feature the echoes of gunfire or the shaping sound of lullabies? The great armistices made by military men or the peacemaking of women in homes and neighborhoods? Will what happened in cradles and kitchens prove to be more controlling than what happened in congresses? When the surf of the centuries has made the great pyramids so much sand, the everlasting family will still be standing, because it is a celestial institution, formed outside telestial time. The women of God know this.[3]

Why is this? What is there about a women's instinctive nature that seems more pointed heavenward? Why do so many more women revel in spiritual realms while so many men struggle to simply keep their natural man at bay?

The Family: A Proclamation to the World provides some clues. "By divine design, fathers are to preside over their families in love and righteousness and are responsible to provide the necessities of life and protection for their families. Mothers are primarily responsible for the nurture of the children. In these sacred responsibilities, fathers and mothers are obligated to help one another as equal partners."

The word *preside* has sometimes been a source of great misunderstanding. Recently, a young father sat in my office and described some ongoing marriage differences he had with his wife. One of his concerns was that his wife struggled to accept his "patriarchal role" when it came to decision making. This role, he explained, was similar to the way a bishop or stake president "presides." "They listen to input from their counselors, then make the big decisions," he explained.

Turning to the family proclamation I had read the paragraph quoted above. I then asked him a series of questions.

"As you understand it, what is your role?" I asked.

"Preside, provide, and protect," he said quickly.

"Exactly," I responded. "But what does it mean to preside?"

He thought for a moment, and then returned to his bishop as the example. "Again, my bishop presides in the ward. He listens to others' opinions, then makes the decision."

"Even if others disagree?"

He nodded. "Sometimes you have to do that when you preside."

I then pointed to the following line in the proclamation, "fathers and mothers are obligated to help one another as equal partners."

I then asked, "Is the bishop an 'equal partner' with his counselors?"

The young father thought for a moment. "No, he's not."

"True. What about the stake president?"

"No, he isn't either."

"Exactly," I responded. "So, in the case of husbands and wives, the word *preside* must mean something else."

Together we researched priesthood responsibilities in the scriptures. We finally concluded that the best alternative way to define "preside" would be "watch over" (D&C 20). We felt like a priesthood holder should be a "watchman on the tower," watching over the home.

I then asked, "So if you are to preside by watching over and your wife is an equal partner, then what does that say about her role as the nurturer?"

When he looked unsure, I continued, "Can I suggest that if you are to be equal partners, as the Lord is suggesting, that the role of watching over (presiding) is on equal footing with nurturing within the home and family?"

I then gave this analogy: Image a fortress in the wilderness with two equal leaders. One is responsible for maintaining the outward defenses. He makes sure the walls are strong and adequately defended. He also has responsibility to keep watch for attacking armies and anything else that might threaten the fort's security.

The other leader is responsible for all the daily activities within the fort. She is more attuned to the needs of all those living within and keeps everything organized. She is sensitive to individual struggles and finds ways to help.

When there are major decisions to be made, equal input from both leaders are required. Resolutions include both the fort's external security needs and the individual inside concerns.

It is this dual need the family proclamation addresses so well. And the reason why nurturing is on equal footing with presiding (watching over).

Divine Nature

The Lord has endowed women with sacred spiritual gifts that aid in the critical nurturing role. One gift is the unique and divine female nature given to daughters of Eve. It is this nature, the deepest desires of a woman's heart, that lead to love and service. Perhaps this nature is best seen in the book of Proverbs.

Hebrew, like many other languages, has both masculine and feminine nouns. Three, however, are specifically identified in scripture as female:

- Wisdom (Proverbs 1:20) "*Wisdom* crieth without: *she* uttereth her voice in the streets."
- Understanding (Proverbs 8:1) "Doth not wisdom cry? And *understanding* put forth *her* voice?"
- Mercy (Alma 42:23) "Also *mercy* claimeth all that which *her* own. . . ."

These three attributes, given female voice, represent a beautiful sampling of divine nature of womanhood. Wisdom appears so often in the Old Testament that it is identified by many Old Testament scholars as Lady Wisdom. To read Proverbs 8, written in Wisdom's first person voice, is to read of her power and effect over the "children of men."

> Counsel is mine, and sound wisdom; I am understanding: I have strength
> > By me kings reign, and princes decree justice.
> > By me princes rule, and nobles, even all the judges of the earth
> > I love them that love me; and those that seek me early shall
> find me.

She also identifies how long she's been involved with mankind:

> The Lord possessed me in the beginning of his way, before his works of old.
> > I was set up from everlasting, from the beginning, or ever the earth was.

When there were no depths, I was brought forth; when there were no fountains abounding with water.

Before the mountains were settled, before the hills was I brought forth:

When he prepared the heavens, I was there.

Finally, there is not much doubt just how much the Lord values her.

Then I was by him, as one brought up with him: and I was daily his delight, rejoicing always before him:

Rejoicing in the habitable part of the earth; and my delights were with the sons of men.

Now therefore hearken unto me, O ye children: for blessed are they that keep my ways. (Proverbs 8:14–32)

As part of divine womanhood, Wisdom, Understanding, and Mercy would seem to create an ideal foundation for the nurturing role given to wives and mothers.

Well, then, did Emily Woodmansee put these sentiments into verse:

The errand of angels is given to women, and this is a gift that, as sisters, we claim:

To do whatsoever is gentle and human, to cheer and to bless in humanities name.

How vast is our purpose, how broad is our mission, if we but fulfill it in spirit and deed.

Oh, naught but the Spirit's divinest tuition, can give us the wisdom to truly succeed.[4]

Elder Jeffrey R. Holland might have put it best when he said,

Be a woman of Christ. Cherish your esteemed place in the sight of God. He needs you. *This Church needs you.* The world needs you. A woman's abiding trust in God and unfailing devotion to things of the Spirit have always been an anchor when the wind and the waves of life were fiercest. I say to you what the Prophet Joseph said more than 150 years ago: "If you live up to your privileges, the angels cannot be restrained from being your associates."[5]

Women and Marriage Communication

Given those natural spiritual propensities, ladies, you are eternally well positioned to greatly assist in bringing the power of the Spirit into marriage relationships. Certainly, my counseling office is more likely to be filled with women eager to see changes in their marriages.

Does this mean that most men don't care about that relationship? Certainly not! But they are less likely to seek outside help (me) to do so. In addition, they are much more disposed to want to "fix" the problem by simply doing more and helping more.

An old joke states that men marry women hoping they'll never change. They want them to forever remain the woman they married. On the other hand, women marry men hoping to change them!

Ladies, the reality is that most men are the great guys you married. But, as men, we need and require the softening and smoothing of the rough edges that only a loving wife can bring. When the Lord declared to Adam, "It is not good for man to be alone," He meant it! It is not good for man to be alone!

Men alone, without the balancing power of a nurturer, so often struggle! If you question that wisdom, simply look at most bachelor apartments—then leave quickly. They can be scary places! The need of the proverbial "woman's touch" is ever present.

This "woman's touch" is the much-needed husband whisperer addition to an eternal marriage and healthy relationships. This whispering process is the loving, peacegiving role of nurturer that makes you so naturally susceptible to spirituality.

This foreordained nurturing gift heals and strengthens. It is intended to bring tenderness and bonding power to a couple. It can provide a "peace, be still" encouragement to a stormy home or an angry husband.

Notes

1 "US Congregational Life Survey—key findings," 29 October 2003.

2 Neal A. Maxwell, "Women of God," *Ensign*, May 1978; italics added.

3 Ibid.

4 Emily Woodmansee, "As Sisters in Zion," *LDS Hymns*, 309.

5 Jeffrey R. Holland, "To Young Women," *Ensign*, November 2005.

4

CONTRITE OR CONTRARY: THE AMAZING POWER OF MEEKNESS

I n looking at the transforming power of whispering, you need to remember that whispering is simply the power of divine meekness applied specifically to your relationships. It changes both the volume and the tone of communication within a marriage and within a home. It is speaking as heaven speaks.

With this in mind, it is also important to determine what whispering is not.

First, Whispering Is Not Passive

During the Savior's earthly ministry, there was some discussion among the disciples about when He would return to the earth. He had warned them that the Second Coming would be a sudden event, catching most people by surprise as they lived regular lives. For instance, he explained, "In the days of Lot, they did eat, they drank, they bought, they sold, they planted, they builded" right up to the moment "that Lot went out of Sodom."

Then the Savior added this insightful warning: "Remember Lot's wife" (Luke 17:28–32).

Remember Lot's wife? What should we remember? That she turned into a pillar of salt for turning around and looking when she wasn't supposed to? That a moment of weakness was a death sentence for this woman?

This scriptural warning tells us the problem with Lot's wife was much more than a moment of disobedience. A careful reading tells us that this wasn't the harsh punishment of a woman whose life was exemplary and then ended when she had a momentary lapse of minor disobedience.

The Lord cautions about the behavior of Lot's wife by explaining that when He comes again, you will need to immediately, without delay, leave your "stuff in the house" and "not return back." The Lord's injunction to you, using Lot's wife as an example, is to not go back, even for your stuff. You should keep going straight ahead. Apparently, Sister Lot hesitated and then placed herself back in danger after being taken by the hand and rescued. Perhaps she even doubted that the cities really would be destroyed.

So the Lord is reminding you not to go backward. In other words, when the time comes to act—act! When an angel takes you by the hand—move!

If you are in the act of urging and encouraging your husband and family, you will not need to be passive but proactively helping things get done and helping them move forward. Nor will you quietly sit by while family members are being destructive or hurtful. Bad behavior needs to be addressed and confronted. Nurturing suggests intervening gently and quickly, but firmly.

This approach is the essence of "reproving betimes [immediately] with sharpness" and then "showing forth afterwards an increase of love toward him whom thou has reproved" (D&C 121:43). That immediate reproving is not passive nor is it weak. Neither is it loud and angry!

Second, Whispering Is Not Fixing

There is a world of difference between loving and enabling. Loving involves setting strong boundaries between what is right and what is not. Loving means holding people accountable for their actions and not sheltering them from consequences.

Enabling (or fixing), on the other hand, means allowing someone to be self-destructive and not intervening for fear of them becoming upset with you. Enabling means more interested in being liked than helping someone grow. It also means making it comfortable enough for them to repeat their bad judgment by shielding them from the consequences of their actions.

Third, Whispering Is Not Silent

When someone wants permission from you to do something, silence implies consent—whether you agree or not! You may think that "the look" or a "cold stony silence" should tell your husband that you disagree with his decision to work on the car's transmission in your kitchen. In all likelihood, you base that idea on the view that *you* would recognize "the look" as disapproving and do something different. *He*, on the other hand, is probably deep into his "car guy" mode and may interpret "the look" from you as "she's really tired and needs a nap and will really be glad when I finally fix the transmission."

Speaking gently is not silent. It is speaking up in a way that cannot be misunderstood by clearly explaining difficulties as you see them. It is making your insights and concerns known and accounted for in a moment of decision making.

Fourth, Whispering Is Not Manipulation

Next, whispering is not a way to manipulate your way through marriage. It is not a "bat your eyes and flaunt your female weakness" to get your way by appealing to your "big strong man." This demeans you and weakens your role in the marriage. Whispering is not guilting him into doing what you want him to do.

As a side note, whispering also does not include using intimacy as a reward or punishment. It is not a payoff for doing the right thing. Martial intimacy was intended by the Lord to increase love and bonding between husband and wife. When used as an inducement for other things, such as home improvement and improved behavior, it makes you the gatekeeper of the rewards and increases the possibility of resentments and anger.

That said, increased gentleness and nurture might easily improve the frequency of shared, loving intimacy. (And of course that will come as very good news in some households!) When spouses are more loving to one another, physical expression becomes a nature outgrowth of that extra attention and caring. It ceases then to be a chore or a checklist item or a prize.

Finally, Whispering Is Not the Art of Gently Winning Every Argument

The art of remaining teachable yet nurturing others in the right direction is a delicate balance. The key to that balance lies in fully developing a broken heart and contrite spirit. As you become more of a "child, submissive, meek, humble, patient, full of love, willing to submit to all things which the Lord seeth fit to inflict upon [you]" (Mosiah 3:19), your heart softens to the point where the Lord can begin a spiritual transformation. Heaven can then whisper to you before you whisper to others. You are taught what to teach before you teach others.

Without the Atonement's transformation, learning to interact more humbly, more gently, and more firmly might be seen as manipulative and insincere. And, indeed, it might be! Without the "mighty change" Alma speaks of (Alma 5:12), your whispering might result in you simply becoming more passive or enabling.

On the other hand, when your heart is mild and meek, it reflects in all you do and say. You deal with those around you with a quiet sincerity. This honest, non-judgmental earnestness opens the hearts of those you whisper to.

One of the Quorum of the Twelve recently visited our stake. Following his remarks, he invited the children of the stake to line up where they could shake his hand. I had an assignment in the meeting and was therefore on the stand. At the conclusion of the meeting, the children rushed forward in such numbers that it was literally impossible to exit the stand.

This meant that, for over thirty minutes, I stood and watched this loving apostle interact with each child that eagerly came up to meet him. His demeanor toward them was loving and gentle. As they approached he leaned forward to listen carefully to the things they would say to him. He smiled warmly and returned their love and occasional hugs. It was easy to see, from a short distance, that he was fully engaged with them. They responded in kind, with huge grins and happy hearts as they bounced off the stand to their waiting—and thrilled—parents.

In relatively short encounters, he had provided a heavenly whisper to them, born of obvious love and concern for their welfare. The spirit he radiated was comfortable and inviting. As I watched, I thought, *What a powerful example of a meek yet influential way of treating people.* I say people, because the way he interacted with children was no different than his approach with the adults and leaders he spoke with over the course of the weekend.

True whispering becomes effective as it reflects a change of heart. This apostle's powerful impact on those children was outward reflection of his role as a servant and witness of the Savior. It was not an act or a technique. It was simply an expression of his love, comfortably reflecting the Savior's love he'd been filled with during his own preparation and a life of service.

After watching him, you might be led to ask, how do you do that? When you examine your daily struggles to treat people in a Christlike manner, does it seem attainable or does it feel completely too far distant? Do you have your good days and start to hope, only to then have your "bad" moments and fear you'll never get there?

Fear

One simple question to ask yourself about this daily struggle might be: what are you afraid of?

One BYU scholar explained how a friend of his had expressed how deeply disappointed she was that the Church did certain things in ways she disagreed with. As he explained it, "The implicit definition of truth she was using was 'If it is truth, why doesn't it live up to my personal ideals and what I want from people and from God?' Also 'if it is the truth, why doesn't it live up to my present concept of perfection?' given the unspoken [and incorrect] assumption that I am perfectly capable of judging and recognizing perfection right now."

He concluded with:

The sacrifice of a broken heart involves putting at risk *what we desire.* The *sacrifice of a contrite spirit* involves putting at risk *what we think,* what seems reasonable. These two sacrifices correspond directly to the figures of Fear and Desire that everywhere stand as temple guardians in the ancient world. Fear is what we think. Desire is what we want. . . . I once studied over seventy reasons that biblical peoples gave to justify the rejection of biblical prophets. Eventually, I realized that they all boil down to people saying, "It's not what I want. It's not what I think."[1]

President Joseph F. Smith echoed this idea when he explained that a critical part of eternal happiness involves the "education of our desires." That education requires the willing (and often painful) sacrifice of what I want, or what I thought would make me happy, in favor of what the Lord wants for me. To do that I have to be willing to give up my ideas of what I think is right, in favor of what the Lord knows is right for me. And that is an education process that requires my willingness to sacrifice my intellectual beliefs, my sins, my future plans, and even my fears.

Ask yourself these questions:
- Do I believe God is my Heavenly Father?
- Do I believe I am His child?
- Do I believe He loves me?
- Do I believe He wants the best for me?
- Do I believe He sees my future?
- Do I believe that His future plan for me is better than my future plan for me?

- Do I believe He is willing to prompt and guide me toward His better plan for me?
- If I believe He is my father, loves me, and wants the best for me, and that His plan for me is infinitely better than any plan I have for me, why do I cling so tightly to my plans and desires? What am I really afraid of?

When I ask clients this question, I almost always hear the same answers:

- I'm afraid He is going to ask me to do something I don't want to do.
- He's going to ask me to change and do something different. And I'm not sure I want to do that.
- He's not going to let me have something I really want.
- He's going to send me more trials—and I don't think I can take much more!

In other words, you think you know the things that would make you happy in this life. When you visualize you, in the future, having achieved or acquired them, you can imagine being really happy or successful. You see that future moment in full color, perhaps with a full movie sound track! You see the wonderful look on your face. In that moment, it looks and feels as if true happiness has happened and your life is now complete.

And you might be right.

Coming back to the reality of right now, you look around and see that all the things—in the present—do not match the hopeful happiness of future. This gap, the one between your current life and the life you visualize in the future, can create the driving discontent that moves you forward. If you believe this future is attainable, you set out to achieve or acquire those things.

Recently I visited with a good friend of mine who is in his first job as a physician. He looked back over his struggle to get good grades in college, get accepted to a medical school (barely), his scrape and scramble to finally get the residency in the field he wanted, and then his ultimate battle to complete his boards and get his license. It was a long and winding battle to reach the finish line.

During the course of his education and training, a future vision burned brightly in his brain: the one of him holding his newly minted MD license and beginning his career as a doctor. Life would be good: no more hoops to jump through, no more classes to pass. Just smiling patients and a great income for the rest of his career!

However, on the day he finally held that license, he was surprised that the thrill he'd hoped to feel, over the course of all those long and painful years was just not there. Tried as he might, there was a level of letdown he had not anticipated.

Is this all there is? he thought at that moment. *Is this it?*

Ultimate happiness comes as you follow the Lord's guidance along his chosen path. You cling to God's iron rod for you, along the plan that is in your best interest. For my friend, no doubt he had received spiritual confirmation in his desire to become a doctor. He could easily point out the times and places where the Lord had intervened in his behalf and opened doors that should have been closed to him. He had followed the Lord's counsel.

However, his assumption was that happiness comes from following the Spirit, and that this was going to be also true in his practice as a physician. In truth, this will probably turn out to be true. However, the Lord's happiness for him has yet to be completely revealed and that could easily come in ways he has yet to even anticipate. At the moment, all he knows is that the complete joy he expected has not yet occurred. He is pleased to be done, but underwhelmed by his own reactions.

A broken heart and contrite spirit means that you are willing to place your desires on the altar of sacrifice. As you do so, you will find yourself saying, "Lord, all I want is what you want!" As Elder Enzio Busche beautifully explained, "With this fulfillment of love in our hearts, we will never be happy anymore just by being ourselves or living our own lives. We will not be satisfied until we have surrendered our lives into the arms of the loving Christ, and *until He has become the doer of all our deeds and He has become the speaker of all our word.*"[2]

This changed spirit allows the Savior to become the "speaker of all our words," thus speaking as He would speak and speaking as only He would. It changes our focus as well as our desires.

Notes

1 Kevin Christensen, *Hindsight on a Book of Mormon Historical Critique,* FARMS Review: Volume 22, Issue 2, 94.

2 F. Enzio Busche, "Truth Is the Issue," *Ensign*, November 1993; emphasis added.

5

OF DRAGGLE-WINGED ANGELS

So, a soft answer turneth away wrath, eh? Tell that to my kids who are being bullied. Tell that to those watching the Savior cleaning out the temple with a whip! In this world, I'm afraid that meek is code word for being fleeced!

Ever had thoughts like that? Or . . .

I can never get this right! I lose my temper or I get frustrated and say something dumb. Even the dog knows to hide from me when I get too stressed out. It's a good thing the Relief Society can't hear me at bedtime!

Learning to be a true whisperer is certainly a process. Said the Prophet Joseph Smith, "Thy mind, O Man [and we may add O Woman as well], if thou wilt lead a soul unto salvation, must stretch as high as the utmost Heavens, . . . How much more dignified and noble are the thoughts of God, than the vain imaginations of the human heart, none but fools will trifle with the souls of men."

On those days when you feel less than ideal, the thought of leading a soul to salvation may seem a long ways off—even laughable! And yet, as Elder Holland reminds us, "Imperfect people are all God has ever had to work with. . . . But he deals with it."[1] Helpmeets and husband whisperers will always be imperfect but vital to the process of softening the world's harshness.

But it can be your imperfections that can haunt you, flashing in your memory as constant reminders of the "stupids" you've stumbled through in your lives. That's why you should take great comfort in the words of the wonderful Scottish preacher George McDonald, the mentor of C. S. Lewis. Speaking of imperfect people he said,

> Come to God, then, my brother, my sister, with all thy desires and instincts, all thy lofty ideals, all thy longing for purity and unselfishness, all thy yearning to love and be true . . .
>
> Come to him with all thy weaknesses, all thy shames, all thy futilities; with all thy helplessness over thy own thoughts; with all thy failure, yea, with the sick sense of having missed the tide of true affairs;
>
> Come to him with all thy doubts, fears, dishonesties, meannesses, paltrinesses, misjudgments, wearinesses, disappointments, and stalenesses:
>
> Be sure he will take thee and all thy miserable brood, *whether of draggle-winged angels, or covert-seeking snakes, into his care.*[2]

On your best days you are draggle-winged angels; angels to be sure, but dragging your tattered spiritual wings behind you. You seek the reassurance that the God you worship is waiting to receive all your miserable brood of personal struggles and to use you in His work of salvation.

The ability to fully see those struggles and yet lean confidently on the power of heaven is the essence of meekness. Said President Harold B. Lee, "The meek man is the strong, the mighty, the man of complete-mastery. He is the one who has the courage of his moral convictions . . . he is the humble minded, he does not bluster."[3]

President Henry B. Eyring tells the story of sitting on a plane with a professional basketball star. In the course of their conversation, President Eyring referred to the classic talk by President Ezra Taft Benson on pride. After listening to the need to be stripped of pride and become humble, the basketball player responded, "I'd get killed if I did that on the court!"[4] In other words, meek is weak and I wouldn't survive!

Yet somehow, someway, it is the meek who end up inheriting the earth. It is the meek who experience the transforming power and influence that comes only by gentleness and meekness and love unfeigned (D&C 121:41). So, you might ask, where and how is this great power in being meek? How do you do this without being run over in a fallen and competitive world? More important, how do you do this with a preoccupied husband or surly teens?

The healing power of meekness rests on two critical pillars: conviction and firmness.

Conviction

In writing from the Liberty Jail, the Prophet Joseph Smith explained that the power and influence that changes the hearts happens only "by persuasion, by long-suffering, by gentleness and meekness, and by love unfeigned; by *kindness and pure knowledge.*" These attributes first change us because they "greatly enlarge the soul *without hypocrisy*" (D&C 121:41–42; italics added).

Draggle-winged angels, so aware of their own faults, might hesitate to make a stand on critical issues. *Who am I to judge?* In addition, declaring something to be right or wrong might offend! So, fearful of judging and faced with a knowledge of their own weaknesses, conviction of what needs to happen can begin to waver like a sapling in a hurricane.

The good news is that standing by your convictions does not require a sinless life! On the contrary, it bears testimony of your complete reliance on the Author of your convictions. It is He who has filled your soul with life-giving truths.

In his letter from Liberty, Joseph warned,

> How vain and trifling have been our spirits, our conferences, our councils, our meetings, our private as well as public conversations— too low, too mean, too vulgar, too condescending for the dignified characters of the called and chosen of God, according to the purposes of His will, from the foundation of the world! We are called to hold the keys of the mysteries of those things that have been kept hid from the foundation of the world until now.[5]

Recently I talked to a sweet single mom who was finding little comfort in this knowledge. She had a teenage daughter who worked hard to make herself difficult to love. She was ungrateful, sarcastic, and willfully breaking every commandment she could think of. It seemed as if her single goal in life was to make her mom as miserable as possible—and she was very good at it!

Mom, in turn, was frequently getting angry, saying a lot of things in retaliation that she later regretted. Her gospel knowledge taught her enough to know that her irate responses to this destructive daughter only made things worse. Her guilt of her own rebellious teen years only added to her misery—and her suspicion that her daughter's contrary nature was somehow her fault.

Brother Hinckley! I know better! I know what I'm supposed to do and I say those terrible things instead! What kind of mother am I? I'm no better than she is! But she makes me so mad sometimes!

Over time, this struggling mom found that she didn't have to waver in teaching her daughter what was right and wrong. She also found, though, that it could be done more softly than she had been doing.

Confident whispering becomes almost impossible when you lack knowledge and conviction. If you are not sure what you know, you will waver and waffle. Then, when criticism comes, you second-guess yourself and either yell back or lapse into silence. As a result, you might be tempted to abandon the castle walls just as the enemy is attacking.

Learning, especially gospel knowledge, leads to greater understanding of what is needed and your role in the plan. It will fill you with increased confidence and the peace that comes from knowing what needs to happen. It sweeps away insecurity and doubt, replacing it with grace and gratitude. Wavering is replaced by wisdom.

As one old sage put it,

He who knows not, and he knows that he knows not,
Is simple—teach him!
He who knows, and knows not that he knows
Is asleep—wake him!
He who knows not, and knows not that he knows not,
Is a fool—shun him!
But he who knows, and knows that he knows
Is wise—follow him.

As you learn and gain greater knowledge, you are worth following. As the psalmist vows, "I will run the way of thy commandments, when thou shalt enlarge my heart" (Psalm 119:32). You should take great comfort in the promise that kindness and pure knowledge will greatly enlarge your soul—without hypocrisy. And that knowledge stiffens the spiritual spine.

Gaining greater knowledge always begins with obedience to temple covenants and commandments. As you do, "then shall thy confidence wax strong in the presence of God" (D&C 121:45).

But I try to be more confident! And it just doesn't work!

It is interesting to note that this verse about confidence in the Doctrine and Covenants is preceded by a familiar, but much misunderstood line. The Lord explains, also in verse 45, that godly confidence comes as we let "virtue garnish [our] thoughts unceasingly." We are at first tempted to read this as referring to moral cleanliness. However, the 1828 Webster's Dictionary defines virtue as strength and power. More to the point, it is seen as godly power.

In addition, to *garnish* is to "clean out or empty," as in the garnishment of wages. Therefore, if we were to "translate" verse 45 in those terms, we might say, "let God's power cleanse your thoughts unceasingly, then shall thy confidence wax strong in the presence of God." In other words, it is *His power* that will clean from our minds the depreciating thoughts of our draggle-winged angels that cause us to hesitate on standing firm on our convictions.

Part of that work of cleansing is to be at peace that any past "stupids" on your part have been forgiven and your nature is being changed. When that happens, you no longer have to carry the worry that you're somehow unqualified or a hypocrite for defining what needs to be done.

If you can allow him to do that for you, you will be filled with greater heavenly confidence. You will be able to softly, clearly—and confidently—be unmoved on what is right and what is not.

Firmness

In his history, Joseph Smith talked about the persecutions he experienced after telling the world about the First Vision. Always a painful memory, he wrote of that experience:

> And though I was hated and persecuted for saying that I had seen a vision, yet it was true; and while they were persecuting me, reviling me, and speaking all manner of evil against me falsely for so saying, I was led to say in my heart: Why persecute me for telling the truth? I have actually seen a vision; and who am I that I can withstand God, or why does the world think to make me deny what I have actually seen?
>
> For I had seen a vision; I knew it, and I knew that God knew it, and I could not deny it, neither dared I do it; at least I knew that by so doing I would offend God, and come under condemnation. (JS—H 1:25)

Doubtless you don't have the experiences that Joseph Smith did. But as your knowledge grows, you do come to understand certain truths and convictions. Whispering is the art of quietly defending those truths in a *firm* and effective way.

And the most effective way I've found to remain firm in a discussion is the combination of two powerful techniques: Fogging and Broken Record. Let me explain them and then use them in an example.

Fogging is the use of simple, noncommittal phrases that communicate two things to another person: One, I heard what you are telling me and, two, I may or may not agree with you. We are hearing but not having to pass judgment on the truthfulness of what they are saying.

Here are a few of my favorite Fogging phrases:

That may be true . . .

I can see how you might believe that . . .

Probably,

Isn't that horrible?

Yes, I probably am . . .

I know it feels that way . . .

You're probably right . . .

That could be . . .

I know . . .

Sure sounds that way, doesn't it?

In each case, the use of a fogging phrase prevents you from having to justify or defend or explain things that you believe don't need to be explained. *You do not have to defend the indefensible!* You know what is right and you carry a quiet conviction that prevents you from having to defend what you know to everyone who comes along.

For instance, you are approached by an elderly lady in the grocery store. She points to the several gallons of ice cream in your cart and says,

Her: You know all that ice cream is unhealthy for you.

You: Well, you see, I'm actually on a diet. I haven't had any ice cream for three months, and, since my daughter is coming into town, I wanted to get some for her so I chose the ones I wouldn't eat and I'm actually going to . . .

And you realize you're explaining yourself, in detail, to someone you don't owe an explanation to. Try this approach instead.

Her: You know all the ice cream is unhealthy for you.
You: I know. Horrible, isn't it?

See, isn't that much better? Fogging says (nicely) I'm not going to debate this with you.

Broken Record is a phrase line that is repeated over and over until the expected behavior occurs or changes. It is a statement of what you will do or someone else needs to do. It is taken from the old record players that would continually repeat the same line over and over until the needle was moved to another part of the record. Like the repeating message on the record player, you simply cling to that line until the desired change occurs.

In order to demonstrate how this works, lets combine both Fogging and Broken Record in a sample dialogue.

Fourteen-year-old daughter: Mom, everyone is going to the mall tonight. Can I go?

Mom: Honey, you haven't finished your homework. You need to stay home and do it.

Daughter: I'll do it when I get home.

Mom: We agreed weeks ago you'd always do your homework first. You need to stay and do your homework.

Daughter: Mom! All my friends are going!

Mom: That may be true, but you need to do your homework.

Daughter: Don't be so mean!

Mom: I know it feels like that, but you need to do your homework.

Daughter: You're just afraid I'm going to get into trouble.
Mom: Probably. But you need to do your homework.
Daughter: Please! I'll do the all the laundry for a week!
Mom: Thanks for the offer. But you need to do your homework.

Mom and daughter have an established agreement. She will finish all homework before going off to the mall. And rather than renegotiate or defend herself for the decision, Mom needs to stand by it. That exact moment is not the time to renegotiate what needs to be done on a school night—it just needs to be followed. Fogging and Broken Record prevent having to defend, repeatedly, what needs to be done or heard at the moment.

Here's another example:

Mike: So if I buy the car, how much will the monthly payments be?
Salesman: It's a great deal. Only $250 a month.
Mike: But when we started, I told you I wouldn't pay more than $200 a month.
Salesman: But this car beat everything else in its class. Especially when you add the tinted windows.
Mike. That may be true. But I'm not going to pay more than $200 a month.
Salesman: I talked to my manager. We can pull some strings to get it down to $245 a month. It's a great deal!
Mike: It may be. But I'm not going to pay more than $200 a month.
Salesman: Mike, nobody in town is going to beat this price!

Mike: I'm sure that's true. But I'm not going to pay more than $200 a month.

Salesman: I don't think you understand just how low we've already gone!

Mike: Very true. But I'm not going to pay more than $200 a month.

Firmness means standing firm on conviction without needing to argue or become angry. Fogging and Broken Record are just two ways of doing it. The alternative is defending or explaining what we shouldn't have to explain. The wonderful thing about Fogging and Broken Record is that it can be done without ever raising a voice or retreating from rules.

Always remember that when our own insecurities are talking, whispering can be replaced by mumbling and boundaries can be washed away with endless people pleasing. Heaven is our standard. The still, small voice does not doubt or compromise. It communicates truth quietly but firmly. True loving whispering does the same thing.

Notes

1 Jeffrey R. Holland, "Lord, I Believe," *Ensign*, May 2013.

2 George McDonald, *Unspoken Sermons*, "Light" (London: Longman, Green and Co., 1889), 172.

3 *Teachings of the Presidents of the Church: Harold B. Lee* (Salt Lake City: The Church of Jesus Christ of Latter-day Saints, 2000), 203.

4 Henry B. Eyring, "I Am a Child of God," BYU Speeches, October 1997.

5 "Section 121: Constitution of the Priesthood," *Doctrine and Covenants Student Manual* (Salt Lake City: The Church of Jesus Christ of Latter-day Saints, 2002), 295.

6
BETTER ANGELS

As Abraham Lincoln prepared his second inaugural address, the bloody Civil War was finally winding down. It was easy to see that the work of rebuilding a weary nation would soon begin in earnest. But death and losses on both sides had left the nation divided and wary of one another. Addressing American citizens on both sides, he stood and pled, "We are not enemies, but friends. We must not be enemies. Though passion may have strained, it must not break our bonds of affection. The mystic chords of memory will swell when again touched, as surely they will be, *by the better angels of our nature.*"

Ah, those better angels, as opposed to the draggle-winged kind. The best part of you. It is those mystic chords—probably premortal—that swell so brightly when touched by the Spirit. They were shaped by endless years of peace and growth, before "there were no fountains abounding with water. Before the mountains were settled, before the hills" (Proverbs 8:24–25).

So, your true nature, your better angel, naturally seeks the "peaceable things of the kingdom" (D&C 39:6). When you are most in tune, you are most at peace.

Well, you've obviously never been to my house on a Sunday morning just before church. Those angels are nowhere to be found, I'll tell you that! And don't even get me started about Family Home Argument on Monday nights. . . .

True! At times, those angels might seem to be taking a vacation. Worse yet, you might think your angels have surrendered and joined the other side! Yet what is the number one response I get from mothers when I ask what they want most? Less fighting. No bickering. They will take a cluttered house and undone dishes—they just want a family that gets along and "then thy servant shall be content!" (Moses 1:36).

You want peace!

When the family proclamation describes a mother's role as being "primarily responsible for the nurture of their children," that nurture is obviously much more than simply putting band-aids on scratches. Whispering nurture, in a family setting, requires "walking the peaceable walk "among your family" especially at times when no one else seems to be doing it!

I get that I'm supposed to be peacemaker. But, the truth is, I'm stressed. I'm tired. I teach Primary. I run my kids to early morning seminary. Can't someone else do the peacemaking thing? At the moment, I'm sure they'll do better than I can.

The truth is that no one can do it better than you can! As a daughter of Eve, you were given a unique set of skills that enable you to do it! That also includes, as we will discuss later, your ability to replenish your emotional health. Peacemaking brings peace to the whisperer as well as the rest of the family!

One of your main assets for your peacemaking journey is the heaven-design of your female brain.

Brainology 101

One roadblock to discovering the better angels of your divine nature is a better understanding of the heavenly devised differences God established between men's brains and women's brains.

Male brains, charged by the Lord with watching over and providing, are more compartmentalized, on average, than is yours. This enables men to exclusively focus on the job at hand by screening out all other distractions. They are able to put out of their minds other responsibilities while completing the task in front of them. True, this focus can be frustrating to you if you need your husband to remember to bring home a loaf of bread after work, but it makes him effective at work.

Because of these different compartments, we tend to function, for instance, as a "husband guy" or a "church guy" when we are in those roles, all the time screening out other responsibilities for a time. When we function as the "work guy," our other roles in life are then placed in the back of brain until they are needed. It is this "one at a time" ability that makes us effective at what we do.

For you, on the other hand, there are no blessed compartments! Every aspect of your life interacts and flows into every other role you have. Your brain operates as one unified and connected entity. If our brain were to look like a building full of separated offices, your brain, in contrast, is more often going to look like the trading floor of the New York Stock Exchange. Every role in your life—mother, wife, daughter, Young Women's leader—reacts to the shouting demands of the others. The downside is that a perceived failure in one shakes your trust in your ability to do one of the others.

A good example of this difference between men's brains and

women's brains comes in our church callings. Typically, a man is called as a bishop for about five years and as a stake president for about ten. After that time, he is pretty worn out and changes are made.

On the other hand, women serve as a Relief Society Presidents or Young Women's presidents for a much shorter period of time. One of the reasons, I believe, is that the structure of a woman's brain makes it harder to let go of the worries and concerns of those you are responsible for. You lie down at night and your brain will not quit! It just keeps processing! As a result, Relief Society Presidents might need the change sooner.

Why does my brain do that? It drives me nuts! Trying to get to sleep can be nightmare—literally!

Actually your brain was designed to do exactly what it does. The membrane that separates both sides of your brain is much thicker than is the male brain. Information flows much more quickly back and forth between the emotional and logical halves of your brain. In addition, your limbic system—your capacity for emotion—is larger and deeper than is ours. The result is that you feel things more deeply and intensely than we do.

Using both sides of your brain to the extent that you do enables you to be far more intuitive than your husband is. As you watch people, for instance, you read their facial expressions, the movement of their eyes. You also hear the tone and volume of their voice, their choice of words, and so on. Because of these things, you read and sense and recognize how others are doing.

Heavenly Father designed you to nurture and so he provided you with all the emotional tools to do it effectively. Deep within your brain cells live the better angels of peacemaking, loving, and gentling. Your soft touch, your gentle words dry a child's tears. They calm the screaming toddler (okay, eventually!). And they can speak encouragement to doubting husbands.

Your divine nature, blessed to work with a marvelously designed brain, is the better angels the Lord needs to bless and serve families and lives in all directions. It was given unique gifts to spot and respond to the needs of people all around you.

However, in today's world, these better angels are also subjected to ridicule and misunderstanding of those who do not see the entire eternal plan. Many may see these nurturing traits as weak when compared with a man's more competitive style. Even within the Church, many women can be seduced by this subtle deception that meekness equals weakness or submission.

Better angels come to learn the great inherent power of whispering meekness. As Elder Maxwell suggested, "The meek go on fewer ego trips, but they have greater adventures. Ego trips, those 'travel now and pay later' indulgences, are always detours."[1]

Now, to this point in this book we've talked about self-whispering and coming to fully appreciate the powerful nature the Lord has entrusted in you. Depending on how your last week has gone, you might see all of this as making perfect sense or completely overwhelming and unattainable!

For the occasionally overwhelmed, can I offer one last critical element necessary for you to embrace the better angels of your nature? Let's look at this example:

Shirley sat dejectedly in my office. Tears streamed down her face as she looked at the different elements of her life and saw only failure. Her teenage daughters were struggling with the Church, and her husband was distant and unhelpful. She felt the full weight of her demanding calling in Young Women and could only see each girl's struggles as her own. In truth, she often felt like running away to where she couldn't be found. She was not sleeping well and had gained twenty pounds in the last six months.

When I asked her who she talked to about her struggles, she just smiled flatly and replied, "No one wants to hear this stuff. No one likes a whiner!"

I thought for a moment and then asked her to read a scripture for me. She rolled her eyes but agreed to do it.

I turned to 1 Nephi 8:24 and asked her to read out loud a verse from Lehi's tree of life vision. She read, "And it came to pass that I beheld others pressing forward, and they came forth and caught hold of the end of the rod of iron; and they did press forward through the mist of darkness, clinging to the rod of iron, even until they did come forth and partake of the fruit of the tree."

"Now," I asked, "when you cling to something, how are you usually feeling?"

She thought for a moment and replied, "If I'm clinging to something, I'm probably pretty scared."

"Exactly," I said, "generally, when are clinging, we are desperate or fearful. Clinging is fear-based. So, with that in mind, now read the next verse."

She read, "And after they had partaken of the fruit of the tree they did cast their eyes about as if they were ashamed."

Shirley looked at the verse for moment and then said, "So they were also afraid of the people in the great and spacious building."

And she was right. We agreed those who had clung to the rod of iron did it out of fear and that the fear of being mocked caused them to fall away "into forbidden paths" (verse 28) and lose what they had at the tree of life.

"Now," I said, "there was another group. Read verse 30."

She read, "behold, He saw other multitudes pressing forward; they came and caught hold of the end of the rod of iron; and they did press their way forward, continually holding fast to the rod of iron, until they came forth and fell down and partook of the fruit of the tree."

Turning to Shirley, I said, "I have two questions for you. First, what is the difference between clinging to the iron rod and 'continually holding fast'?"

She nodded and replied, "I would think that clinging is fear based and continually holding would be faith based."

"Why?"

"Because with clinging they were afraid to let go. They were looking at the rod. With the second group, they were just using the rod to the get to the tree. It seems like it would be about the tree."

"Which is?"

"The tree was the love of God."

"And the tree," I replied, "is also symbolic of the Savior."

She nodded.

"Now, my second question. This second group did an interesting thing. They came forth and fell down and partook of the fruit of the tree. How did they do that? How do you fall down but still eat of the fruit?"

This stumped her. She thought about the fruit perhaps lying on the ground, but that didn't make sense to her. The idea that they had fallen down would certainly make reaching up into the tree much harder.

"Let me give you a hint," I suggested. "What is the tree representative of?"

"The love of God. The Savior."

"Right. And how often do we have times in the scriptures when people would approach the Savior and fall down at His feet?"

"A lot," she replied. "The Nephites did it."

"So, again, how does someone fall down at the tree but still partake of the fruit?"

She stared at me for a moment before it finally hit her. "Oh, I get it!" She said with a grin, "Someone gave it to them!"

I smiled back at her. "There you go. For those who fall down and worship, the fruit is given to them. But how true to life this is for you. You are drowning in the responsibilities of family and callings. You beat yourself up and keep trying harder and then blame yourself when you 'fail.' You keep attempting to do it all by yourself and you're exhausted. You've been clinging!

"In truth, the Lord has never expected you to do all this alone. You have friends, you have leaders, you have the temple, you have the Spirit—all of whom are waiting to help and provide counsel and suggestions. Quit running yourself ragged and let others help!"

The better angels of your nature find counsel and help and solace in a variety of sources. They carry the heavy responsibility of nurturing but they were never intended to do it unaided. They were intended to fall down and worship and be fed by those around you and by the Savior himself. It is this daily manna, touched with gratitude, that invites whispering.

Notes

1 Neal A. Maxwell, "Meekness—A Dimension of True Discipleship," *Ensign*, March, 1983.

7
HELPMEET 101

Elder Russell M. Nelson describes a heartbreaking incident from when he was a heart surgeon.

In 1957, Brother and Sister H. brought their third child to me for repair of congenital heart disease. Their first child had died from congenital heart disease before the advent of cardiac surgery, and their second also died after an unsuccessful open-heart operation that I performed. I operated on the third child, but she died later that night.

My grief was beyond expression. When I went home, I told the story to Dantzel and said, "I'm through. I'll never do another heart operation as long as I live!" I wept most of the night. All I could think of were the faces of those two parents, and could still see those pathetic children in my mind, blue-lipped and with clubbed fingers, yet with smiles of confidence and hope. I determined that my inadequacies would never be inflicted on another human family.

When morning came, Dantzel finally said, "Isn't it better to keep trying than to quit now and require others to go through the same grief of learning what you already know?"

I listened to her counsel. I returned to the laboratory to work a little harder, learn a little more, and strive further.[1]

As the creation of the earth was reaching completion, "I, the Lord God, said unto mine Only Begotten, that it was not good that the man should be alone; wherefore, I will make an help meet for him" (Moses 3:18).

Just what is a *helpmeet*? First of all, we need to understand that the word *helpmeet* is not a single word, it is two: *help* and *meet*. The word "help," in Hebrew, is *ezar*, meaning "to save or succor." The Hebrew for "meet" is *neged*, meaning "in front of," like a mirror, like us.

Therefore, if we rewrite that verse as it was originally intended, it reads, "It was not good that the man should be alone; wherefore, I will send someone who will succor and save him; someone who is just perfect for him, someone who is just like him."

In speaking to young adults of the church, Elder Earl C. Tingey admonished, "You must not misunderstand what the Lord meant when Adam was told he was to have a helpmeet. *A helpmeet is a companion suited to or equal to us.* We walk side by side with a helpmeet, not one before or behind the other. A helpmeet results in an absolute equal partnership between a husband and a wife. *Eve was to be equal to Adam as a husband and wife are to be equal to one another.*"[2]

President James E. Faust agreed, saying, "Every father is to his family a patriarch and every mother a matriarch as coequals in their distinctive roles."[3]

However, the idea of a wife as her husband's helpmeet has been much misunderstood in the minds of some. If she is to eternally be something of a "wingman," a sweet and loving executive secretary and nanny, then we have missed the true nature of the intended relationship.

That sounds good. But the scriptures keep talking about "Adam this" and "Adam that." It seems to be all about Adam! Where is Eve in this picture?

70

It may look that way until we understand the Lord's language. Speaking of Adam, the Lord revealed to Moses, "In the image of his own body, male and female, created he them . . . and called *their* name Adam" (Moses 6:9). And there is the great truth. The name Adam most often describes a plural relationship—Adam and Eve.

Mother Eve

When we look at examples of how to be the kind of helpmeet the Lord intends, it is good to look to the first helpmeet, Mother Eve, as an example.

LDS scholar Valarie Hudson Cassler suggests the following when looking at Eve's role in the Fall and plan of salvation:

> We must ask ourselves what partaking of the fruit of the tree of the knowledge of good and evil means in a spiritual sense. . . . It means to enter into mortality with a mortal body, to enter into full agency, and to have awakened within us the light of Christ that will serve us so well as we pass the veil. Think—two people, two trees— whose stewardship does this sound like? It is through women that souls journey to mortality and gain their agency, and in general it is through the nurturing of women, their nurturing love of their children, that the light of Christ is awakened within each soul. And I would include in that list of souls Jesus the Christ. Even Christ our Lord was escorted to mortality and veiled in flesh through the gift of a woman, fed at his mother's breast, awakened to all that is good and sweet in the world. Women escort every soul through the veil to mortal life and full agency.
>
> I believe that when we think about it—two people, two trees— that what we're really thinking about is two stewardships. And that the fruit of the First Tree symbolizes the gift that women give to every soul that chose the plan of Christ. It symbolizes the role and power of women in the Great Plan of Happiness. It was not, in this

view, right or proper for Adam to partake first of the fruit of the First Tree. It was not his role to give the gift of the fruit of the First Tree to others. It is interesting to think that even Adam, who was created before Eve, entered into full mortality and full agency by accepting the gift of the First Tree from the hand of a woman. In a sense, Adam himself was born of Eve.[4]

Thus, Eve began her helpmeet-*ness* with a full sense she was a complete partner in the plan of happiness. Her contribution was to be equal to her husband's. Her input to decision making was as critical as was his, only her stewardship was different. Each stewardship was symbolized by its own tree in the garden. Each held vital keys, shared by a loving Heavenly Father, essential for exaltation. Understanding this concept gave Eve confidence to draw on every aspect of her spiritual gifts and talents to help them succeed and to support her husband in his new role as tiller of the ground.

Her role as helpmeet was to introduce all living into mortality, then nourish and prepare them for life's challenges. To aid in that stewardship she was given the gifts of wisdom and understanding to draw upon the powers of heaven in fulfillment of her responsibility. Those gifts represented her half of the Adam Partnership, her keys to all mortality.

Get Us Talking

So, I understand I am to be an equal partner here. But if I'm his helpmeet, what does that look like? How do I know when I'm there?

As we talked about in the last chapter, your female brain is divinely designed to nurture. You often solve problems by talking your way through it. This is one reason female friends can be so critical for you. You talk, they listen. They give feedback and listen to your concerns. They help you arrive at a solution. But in the end, it is your solution.

As men, we often do just the opposite. We tend to internalize, to research, and then to stew about possible solutions. We disappear into our "man cave" in order to sort out what to do. Then—and only if necessary—will we finally break down and ask for help and ideas. But we must first be comfortable that we've done all we can do to fix it followed by the frustration of knowing we *should* have been able to fix it!

Recently there was great rejoicing in our house. On a Saturday afternoon, I tackled a difficult home repair project. When it comes to home repair, it is widely known that I am a functionally challenged. Usually my repair jobs require the hiring of a professional to come behind me and do the job over. But in this case, I decided to rise to the challenge.

Cindy cheered me on and wished me luck and, I'm sure, began immediately praying for my success and for the survival of the house. I first went to the home repair super center and carefully selected the right replacements. I met some friends from the stake, who gave helpful advice and directed me to the right aisles. Sometime later I returned home and cautiously began the task. As luck would have it, the job went well—better than I expected—and within a short period of time I proudly brought Cindy in to see my handiwork. Of course she was thrilled and heaped tons of praise on me, marveling at my handyman prowess.

And why wouldn't she? She now had a new doorknob on the front door! The great news is that no one had to come later to reinstall it and it works perfectly. But, on my list of jobs to do, it was a huge risk to my self-esteem and male standing.

However, had the task proven to be harder that expected, my first tendency would have been to retreat back to my man cave/office, search Google, and pray I wouldn't have to ask someone for help, thus exposing my poor home repair skills. Cindy, as my loving helpmeet, provides loving reminders that I can ask for help when I come to those moments.

Helpmeets, we do need your help, allowing us to discuss our feelings, our problems and the solutions we are contemplating. We need you to whisper us into being more transparent with what we are planning. However, please keep in mind that many of us are hesitant to open up because of what we expect your reaction to us will be. Your past responses are critical and may shape just how willing we are to telling you what is on our mind.

One Christian pastor put together a wonderful list of concerns the men in his church were revealing to him as he polled them on marriage communication. In his book, *What Your Husband Isn't Telling You*, David Murrow lists some of these male concerns:

- He wants to be more honest with you, but you often become angry when he tells you how he's really feeling. Many wives innocently train their husbands to conceal the truth from them.
- He's afraid to admit weaknesses or fears, especially to you.
- At work he feels like a genius. At home he's a dunce.
- He's tired of being seen as 100 percent of the problem in the marriage.
- He hates having to read your mind. Tell him clearly what you want and then be happy when you get it.

Much of our early socialization as boys is focused on *not* revealing what we fear or what we're worried about or what we are feeling. *Pick yourself up, rub some dirt on it, and get back in the game!* A nurturing helpmeet provides a place for us to open up but we must overcome all our past training.

Again, how you respond is critical!

Picture, for a moment, that Bob, who is forty-five, comes home and talks again about how much he hates his job. He then announces that he is considering quitting his job as a CPA to become a hot dog vender in New York City.

Honey, it would be less stress and I could enjoy having regular customers. Plus, you know how much I love hot dogs!

His wife, Ann, responds by panicking and locking herself in the bedroom. There she calls all three of her sisters, her mom, and her visiting teacher. She posts a desperate plea for help on Facebook. She also cancels their cable TV as she begins to figure out ways to cut down on their expenses. This all comes during a week of sleepless nights and periodic crying jags.

After watching all this, Bob says two things, one to Ann and one to himself. To Ann, he says, *Honey, I was just having a hard day. I'll be fine. I'm not really going to go sell hot dogs in NYC. That would be stupid! I don't know what got into me.*

Ann smiles and nods gratefully. She then calls her sister and cancels her brother-in-law's emergency trip to come and talk Bob out of being stupid.

But Bob, inside his head says to himself, *I will never again tell her what I'm thinking. Next time I'll keep it to myself!*

And he does.

Helpmeet-*ing* happens when you are able listen without overreacting. Help us explore and talk through all the consequences of that we're thinking. Helpmeet-ing is establishing an openness that enables us to talk and explore and get the input from you we desperately need. It doesn't mean supporting the hot dog venture, but if you'll let us talk it out, we will come to the same conclusion.

Now, to truly do this, you will need to turn off and shut down your "awfulizer."

What is that?

Your awfulizer is a small deadly component of your brain. Unfortunately, it won't show up on an MRI. It takes in a little information, forms a picture, and then magically transforms it into the WORST POSSIBLE SCENARIO imaginable. Little things become huge! Molehills become Alps. For Ann, a short comment about selling hot dogs becomes her preparation for living in poverty and squalor and misery in NYC while Bob lives out his hot dog fantasy.

Well, aren't we supposed to plan for the worst and hope for the best?

Nice idea! The problem is that your awfulizer can cause you to react and plan for the most horrible outcome—with all the emotional reaction as if it has already happened. And while this may seem like good planning, it is also a recipe for anxiety. In addition, you will tend to react out of that anxiety—*you're thinking of WHAT?!*—and cause your husband to share less with you in the future.

Whisper to us. Keep our feet on the ground. Listen to us, then gently help us see that the prices of hot dogs are rising, as is the cost of mustard, and that it just isn't that great a plan. Then invite us to fire up the grill and live out those fantasies in a backyard cookout.

Help Us See Us

As we talked about previously, your wonderful brain can gather an amazing amount of information. While, as husbands, we tend to understand you mainly by simply listening to the words you speak, your brain reaches out to read our facial expressions, our words, the tone of our voice, our inflections, and our nonverbal communications. It also scans our gestures, what we're wearing, how many times we've worn it, whether we shaved, if we missed a spot, our sighs, our squints, our weight, our hairline . . . need I say more?

I often try to explain to men that their wives know them better than they know themselves. You spend a lifetime becoming an expert on us. I tell them, *Your wife will know you are tired before you do*!

Remember, part of being a help*meet* to us is to be the mirror—our mirror—the one like us. For this reason, we need you to reflect back to us what you see and observe.

Please note, though: it makes sense that if this feedback is only seen as critical and judgmental, your observations will be avoided. But if they're expressed with love and permission, they'll be more likely to be received and followed.

Bob, can I point something out?

Sure, Ann. What is it?

Ah, you've worn your favorite shirt to the office four times this week. I wonder if we should at least get it to the dry cleaners before it begins to move around under its own power. . . .

Why thank you Ann for the timely suggestion. I guess I was unaware. Thank you for that insightful observation! Let me quickly change my shirt!

Okay, maybe it won't sound exactly like that—but asking before providing observations usually helps.

Ultimately, you are the helpmeet: the one like us, the one who saves us. Not only do you introduce us into mortality, you nurture us physically, emotionally, and spiritually. Your daily ministrations prepare the soil of our heart to receive the seeds of salvation (Alma 32:28). You do that with the gentle, whispering nurture you were endowed with. You do it with your vast ability to love and deep loyalty to us despite all our stupids! And you do it because you see the world from a different place than we do, one where softness and meekness are strengths and are powerful forces for change.

Truly, when God said, it is not good for man to be alone . . . He meant it!

Notes

1 Lane Johnson, "A Study in Obedience," *Ensign,* August 1982; italics added.
2 Earl C. Tingey, "The Simple Truths from Heaven," CES Fireside, January 13, 2008; italics added.
3 James E. Faust, "The Prophetic Voice," *Ensign*, May 1996, 4.
4 Valarie Hudson Cassler, "The Two Trees," FAIR Conference, 2010.

8

WALK WITH ME: THE ART OF FORGIVENESS

One of the great challenges of whispering in general is the need to extend forgiveness to those who have hurt you. And no forgiveness is more difficult than letting go pain caused by someone you love and care about.

In addition, husband whispering is also much more difficult when you withhold forgiveness from yourself. In both cases, the leavening power of the Spirit is blocked. For this reason, let's look more closely at why forgiving others—and ourselves—whispers peace to our soul.

For Mother Eve, mortality was often a painful place. As the Lord had warned, in much sorrow she brought forth and raised her children. For instance, after seeing so many of her children follow Satan, she'd placed high hopes in her son Cain, saying, "I have gotten a man from the Lord: wherefore he may not reject his words" (Moses 5:16). She could have added, "As most of my other children have!"

But Cain also "loved Satan more than God," and quickly dismissed the Lord's council saying, "Who is the Lord that I should know him?" Pride was already eating away at his heart, blinding him and souring his decisions.

Many of the subsequent generations followed Cain's lead until finally the Lord exclaimed, "Their hearts have waxed hard, and their ears are dull of hearing, and their eyes cannot see afar off" (Moses 6:27)

I think you just described my house every morning before school . . .

Well said! In this case, the Lord did what He always does . . .

Rained fire and brimstone or at least a lot of warnings?

Close. Called an inspired teacher to teach them the gospel. "And it came to pass that Enoch journeyed in the land, among the people; and as he journeyed, the Spirit of God descended out of heaven, and abode with him" (Moses 6:26).

Enoch's response should sound familiar to everyone who's ever been given a calling in the Church or tried to raise hormonally soaked thirteen-year-old contrarians. "Why is it that I have found favor in thy sight?" he asks. *Why me?* And then he lays out his reasoning (as if God didn't already know): I am "but a lad, and all the people hate me!" For proof, he then added, "I am slow of speech!"

In essence, Enoch is trying to explain how surprised he is to have this particular calling. *I am too young, people hate me—and I'm a horrible speaker. You can't mean me! Remember that these people are blind, won't listen, and spend their days plotting murder for gain. I'm the last person they'd ever listen to!*

It is the Lord's response to this boy prophet that should inspire any of us who struggle in the things we are called to do:

Go forth and do as I have commanded thee, and no man shall pierce thee. Open thy mouth, and it shall be filled, and I will give thee utterance, for all flesh is in my hands, and I will do as seemeth me good.

Behold my Spirit is upon you, wherefore all thy words will I justify; and the mountains shall flee before you, and the rivers shall turn from their course; *and thou shalt abide in me, and I in you; therefore walk with me.* (Moses 6:32–34)

We may look at Enoch and believe that we'd probably never need to move a mountain or turn a river. Yet each of us have our own mountains that seem too big, too hard. When we are called on to forgive, gaining the confidence that the Lord is willing to walk with us makes the mountain moving much easier. *If he is there, I suppose I can do it!*

A few years ago I was speaking at a class at BYU about forgiveness. A sister on the third row raised her hand and explained that she'd been abused by a relative when she was a child. "But," she said, "I've forgiven him and I'm now okay."

As she spoke though, large tears ran down her cheeks as she stared back at me.

"Or maybe not?" I gently asked.

"I thought I had forgiven him," she replied tearfully.

I then explained that she'd been greatly hurt and betrayed by someone she trusted. Her tears spoke volumes about the fact that some deep feelings still remained despite her best efforts to remove them.

"Do you possess the ability to clean those painful thoughts and feelings from your brain and heart?" I asked her.

"I thought I did. I've really tried."

We then went on to talk about the powerful cleansing that comes from the Savior through His Atonement.

I concluded, "In the end, only He has the ability remove these feelings from your brain and heart. If He can part the Red Sea, He can cleanse those things from you. However, only He knows you well enough to know when and how He will do it. The hardest part for us is letting Him take over and do what He is anxious to do for us."

For her, those feelings were as impossible to move as mountains were for Enoch. In your daily list of things to do, you also have rivers to turn and mountains to move. Things that seem to be well beyond your natural ability to conquer. Yet the Lord calls you to do it anyway because He both knows the task at hand and the help He will provide you along the way. The Lord's response to your call is exactly the same as it was for Enoch: *walk with me*!

But, as you are constantly reminded, walking with God is no guarantee of a painless journey. In fact, some level of pain seems inevitable. Later in his vision, Enoch watched the horror of the coming Great Flood. He saw the end result of the Lord needing to cleanse the earth of the wickedness that had continued to spread and dominate. He saw Satan with a chain, wrapping the earth in darkness.

Then, to his complete surprise, he turned to see the God of heaven weeping. His immediate response was to remind the Lord that he was surrounded by peace, justice, and love. "How is it thou canst weep?" he asks (Moses 7:31).

In other words, *I don't understand how you, who has perfect knowledge and are surrounded by peace and love, could ever be sad and tearful. Shouldn't Godhood insulate you from that? Those left on the earth during the flood are the truly wicked and will have rejected every chance to repent. They spurned you and your commandments. They kill their fellowmen to get gain. They're really just getting what they deserve, aren't they?*

The Lord's reply serves as a reminder to any who would whisper peace among any of God's children, regardless of their level of obedience. "Behold these thy brethren; they are the workmanship of mine own hands. . . . Wherefore should not the heavens weep, seeing these shall suffer?" (Moses 7: 32, 37).

Because I have perfect love and endless knowledge, I know too well the pain and misery they will go through. They will suffer death here and pain in spirit prison because they wouldn't listen and "misery shall be their doom" (Moses 7:37). And I love them. They are still my children, the workmanship of my hands.

In other words, sometimes that forgiveness will need to extend to those who are too blind and willful to see the pain of their own actions. Yet we are asked to forgive them anyway, mourning at the pain that one day will come their way.

Truthfully, the eternal role of the Spirit is to nurture and whisper change to faulty mortals here on earth. Gentleness helps soften those who are sometimes not very lovable and need most to hear the message of peace. But still it whispers, looking for the right time and place when it will finally help change a heart that was bent on destruction.

In the same way, your ability—as women, as wives, and as mothers—is to nurture, as you've been foreordained to do. Your gentle whispering can breathe the same spirit of change. And that spirit is intended for those who receive that love, but more especially for those who may not yet be.

For instance, husbands can be prideful, stubborn, and ego-driven. And that's just before breakfast. They can become overly absorbed in work or sports or a thousand other distractions. They easily get lost in the "thick of thin things."

You mean like screaming at the TV during a football game? Or spending months researching the right nine iron or newest iPad?

Yes, things like that! We can also do things that are thoughtless and cause you great pain. We say dumb things at the worse possible moments. Now, in all fairness, we do spend a lot of time knowing we did something stupid, but not being quite sure what we did, when we did it, and what to do about it. Thus, we spend time thinking we should fix whatever it was, if only we knew what it was and hoping we'll solve it before we have to admit we did it.

So, yes, you spend a large part of your nurturing time whispering peace to those who have hurt you in some way. This is perhaps the greatest challenge of all—speaking peace to the very people who love you and have hurt you anyway. Your mountain to move just might be not allowing bitterness to creep in and steal your spiritual strength.

President Uchtdorf explains, "Strained and broken relationships are as old as humankind itself. Ancient Cain was the first who allowed the cancer of bitterness and malice to canker his heart. He tilled the ground of his soul with envy and hatred and allowed these feelings to ripen."[1]

It is for these reasons that learning to till and cultivate a spirit of forgiveness becomes paramount to your peacegiving mission. If there is any measure of consolation, God has to do the same thing on a regular basis.

A good example of His forgiveness is found in Jeremiah. Despite constant warnings about their disobedience, those at Jerusalem became more and more destructive. Eventually, prophets like Lehi were forced to flee for their lives. Finally, the Lord allowed Jerusalem to fall to captors in Babylon. Once there, the Jews were being falsely promised that they would soon return to Jerusalem. Tempering those false promises, the Prophet Jeremiah received a revelation explaining that they would remain in captivity for at least seventy years.

But despite their willful wickedness, the Lord also promised that they would return home, saying that He would accomplish "my good word toward you." And despite the fact that their lack of obedience suggested that they deserved little mercy, He extended these hopeful and loving words to them in exile:

> For I know the thoughts that I think toward you, saith the Lord, thoughts of peace, and not of evil, to give you an expected end.
>
> Then shall ye call upon me, and ye shall go and pray unto me, and I will hearken unto you.
>
> And ye shall seek me, and find me, when ye shall search for me with all your heart.
>
> *And I will be found of you*, saith the Lord. (Jeremiah 29:10–14; emphasis added)

To those trapped in the pain of past hurts, the Lord's healing balm may seem a long way off. That pain is certainly magnified if your husband or kids caused it. Years ago, I worked with a young couple who were looking seriously at divorce. Both had been married previously. One of the main areas of contention was a lack of physical intimacy. Try as she might, the wife felt a certain amount of physical revulsion when she thought about making love with him.

In our conversations, she explained that she'd always felt guilty about some incidents of premarital sex shortly before their wedding. It had never been disclosed to their bishop prior their temple marriage. She also disclosed that her soon-to-be husband had been quite pushy and demanding about the physical encounters, and that she'd been angry about being pressured into them.

"But," she explained, "I forgave him years ago, so I don't think that's the problem now."

I then talked to her about another client I had worked with. Years ago she'd been sexually active during her teens and had gotten pregnant. She had then made the best decision for her baby and gave it up for adoption to a wonderful loving couple. She had then worked hard on forgiveness and turned her life around. Years later she married a returned missionary in the temple.

We then talked about how this young girl had sinned, repented, was clean and forgiven, and was now living an exemplary life. But she still had a daughter, whom she had not seen grow up, who was now an adult that she would go visit with occasionally. In other words, forgiveness heals the sin, but it doesn't necessarily shield us from the long-term consequences of our actions.

This sweet wife had "forgiven" her husband of his premarital pressuring, but the guilt and deep resentment still remained within her. And the long-term consequences of unresolved anger were now interfering in her ability to fully engage with him intimately. Her heart had forgiven, but her thoughts and resentments had not yet let go of how she viewed him.

Another factor, though, was her view of herself. She had maintained a high level of self-blame and guilt at having given in to him. While she was still angry at her husband, she was equally appalled at her own behavior. How could things ever be safe if she potentially had such poor judgment.

This good sister was plagued with self-blame as are so many other women in the church. *How can I whisper based on my so-called divine nature when I have so many flaws. What about the days when the real problem in the house is me and my attitude. On those days I'm as far from bringing peace to my home as someone off the street! My whisperer is stuck on "yell," and I can't seem to turn it off.*

Forgiveness is a vital part of husband whispering. And much of that forgiveness is certainly begins with self-forgiveness. Someone once said the first rule of the universe is that we know what it is that we should do, but we don't, in fact, do it!

Bringing the divine spirit of peace into a home or marriage doesn't require perfection now, in the past, and especially in the future. Whispering changes you at the same time as it affects those around you. The messenger is as blessed as the recipient.

Again, the Lord's promise to Enoch, "open thy mouth, and it shall be filled, and I will give thee utterance," is as applicable to you as it was to him. Enoch was realistic about his flaws but chose to trust the Lord and move forward. He did so with a firm belief that it would be heaven's words in his mouth and that the Spirit would guide his actions.

Enoch also didn't wait until he had been perfected. During the 365 years it took for his Zion to be readied for translation, Enoch was in the process of being perfected along with everyone else. Lifting them meant lifting himself. It was his teaching that helped change and perfect him.

President Monson has promised, "When we are on the Lord's errand, we are entitled to the Lord's help. *Remember that whom the Lord calls, the Lord qualifies.*"[2] And that qualification includes transforming you above yourself and aiding you in your efforts to bless those around you.

This occurs because whispering peace requires being filled with a conciliatory spirit, one that softens hearts and melts pride. The vessel that holds peace is also cleansed by that peace. Receiving

His loving image on our countenance (Alma 5) helps provides an example for others to strive for. They see what is possible, through you.

And, yes, your family sees you at your worst as well as at those whispering moments. But they also are gifted to watch a transformation in progress, the visual result of how the spirit softens and deepens our commitment to peace. The eternal calling to nurture means that this marriage and this family will have a healing measure of gentling peace through you—despite your bad days and warts and quirks!

They will also watch as you love and forgive, whispering a conciliatory spirit that encourages repentance in those who have hurt you. This spirit, this love, helps prevent the mistakes of the past from robbing future joy.

Notes

1 Dieter F. Uchtdorf, "The Merciful Obtain Mercy," *Ensign*, May 2012.
2 Thomas S. Monson, "Duty Calls," *Ensign*, May 1996, 44; emphasis added.

9

THE TONGUE OF ANGELS

*S*o, as I understand it, if I'm learning to be a true whisperer, speaking as heaven speaks, I will be speaking softly but firmly. I will be humble and meek without allowing myself to be a passive doormat. My question is this: exactly what am I'm supposed to be whispering? What am I saying?

Learning *how* to whisper also means learning *what* to whisper. You already know that when you are *not* whispering, when you are angry or critical or tired, then what you say is not likely to be a helpful and a gentling influence to your family! And that is putting it kindly. In all honesty, you probably still cringe when you think of past things you might have said in the heat of the moment. If there was a way to take those things back, you would.

All of us would.

In order to whisper, you begin by first listening to the whisperings you hear from the Spirit. The Lord explained to Joseph Smith, "Verily I say unto you, my friends . . . this commandment which I give unto you, *that you shall call upon me while I'm near*" (D&C 88:62; emphasis added). In other words, you are being invited to ask the Lord for help and directions—especially when He is near.

When is God near? Think about times you've sat in a church meeting and heard something inspirational. Maybe you were studying the scriptures or reading an article. You might even have felt something as you were driving, drifting off to sleep, or simply going about your day. The Spirit begins to swell within and you recognize its presence. Perhaps your heart begins beating a bit faster, or you maybe you feel a growing sense of calm or a rising level of gratitude. Heavenly whisperings depend on your unique spiritual gift and how it operates within you. The result is that you know that you are feeling closer to the Spirit.

That is the moment! Talk to Him to your heart's desire. Explain your concerns, your doubts, and your worries. Perhaps your mind has been dwelling on all those things you've been blessed with and your heart is simply swelling with gratitude. Tell Him! Whisper back to Him while He is close.

More important, *listen* while He is close. Regardless of the topic of the meeting or the title of the book you were reading—listen. What do you hear as heaven whispers? What counsel are you getting about yourself or those you love? What solutions begin to form in your mind? What impressions do you get about what you need to discuss with your husband or how to approach a difficult child. What is it you hear?

At those moments, please do not be in a hurry. Perhaps, as you close a prayer, you feel His sweet presence close by. Your heart senses it. A greater peace settles on your mind. When that occurs, linger. Be still. Don't simply rush off noting that you felt His presence. Quietly let that gentle Spirit wash over and fill your heart. Stop what you are doing and avoid the temptation to rush off to other things.

This willingness to wait is critical to hearing the workings—and wordings—of the still, small voice. It was intended to be quiet, dignified, and peaceful. The voice of loving truth always is. It was also meant for you to strain a bit to hear it. As you incline your ears, quiet your mind, and focus your heart, you are placing yourself more in tune with the peace and love that flows so generously from above. He stands at the door and knocks, but it is a quiet tapping at our door.

As you take time to do this, you train yourself to restrain the natural man or woman's tendency to rush by sacred things on its insistent journey back to worldly demands.

It is also in those moments that you will know what to whisper to others and when to do it. Allow the Spirit to teach you the words and phrases that need to be said. These words will be completely different than the ones you've said in the heat of a frustrated moment. They will be firm but affirming.

I love you—but what you did was unacceptable. Lets talk about ways to not repeat it. How can I help you with it?

What you said really hurt my feelings. I'm willing to take responsibility for my actions, but I felt like what you said was unfair and hurtful.

Recently, Cindy and I traveled to Palmyra and visited the Sacred Grove. On a quiet morning, we arose early and walked through that grove of trees just as the sun was rising. After going our separate ways, we lingered and prayed for about two hours.

What surprised me, as I walked in that misty morning stillness, were the sounds. Birds overhead—a lot of birds!—frogs croaking in the small stream, the rustle of small animals through the bushes. I was even aware of the sound of my own heart, filling with joy as I lingered there. It was the quiet sounds that left such a powerful mark on me during that peaceful morning.

During that walk, I also found there was no rush to move on to any other things. I had come with no agenda other than to experience the Lord's presence. I easily dismissed my mind's mental tugging to move on to other things and stayed still. In fact, just the opposite was true—I longed to be able to stay there always.

That experience also reminded me of a divine pattern for learning spiritual truths, one I wish I was better at on a regular basis. As I slowed down, I listened more. As I did, I was quietly fed in a most sacred place. Quieted, I then opened my heart to be taught. When I did, I was soon filled with spiritual assurance from above.

Afterward, I met Cindy outside the grove and we talked of our experiences—in hushed voices. We whispered about what we felt and gratefully recognized a renewed testimony of the truthfulness of what Joseph Smith said happened there. It was true!

Shortly after, we returned home to our busy lives. Waiting for us were crowded agendas and demands on all sides. Our loud and busy world was still there, filling our ears and heads with daily bustle. We drove home from the airport in rush hour traffic and, sadly, the quiet of the grove seemed so far away. But the impact on a grateful heart still remained, long after being there.

There is no question that finding quiet moments to ponder is always a challenge. For instance, resisting the temptation to quickly pray and hop into bed is always a battle: sometimes won but often lost! Yet the Lord's pleadings are clear: "Be still, and know that I am God" (Psalm 46:10).

Hearkening

When you stop and listen, you find out what it is the Lord would have you do and say in your whisperings. The next question is, will you hearken to those promptings? We first learn of the importance of hearkening in the Garden of Eden. After he has eaten of the forbidden fruit, Adam is told that the earth will be cursed "for thy sake" (Genesis 3:17). This is the blessed consequence that came because he "*hearkened* unto the voice" of Eve. Later Eve's consequences would be in childbearing and in hearkening to Adam, provided that he is hearkening to and obeying the voice of God.

In each case, a quick reading would make it sound as if the need to hearken (listen and follow) is a punishment given to both Adam and Eve. Yet the act of hearkening was the greatest blessing given to each of them. For Adam, hearkening to his wife resulted in opening the door for the plan of salvation to begin. It was now available for themselves and for all of Heavenly Father's children. Not hearkening would have destroyed the plan and fulfilled Lucifer's goal for our eternal misery. For Mother Eve, hearkening to her husband meant receiving baptism and the saving priesthood ordinances of the gospel. Not hearkening would have left her—and him—outside the celestial kingdom.

For you, hearkening to the voice of the Lord means learning all you need to know to return to your Heavenly Father. Not hearkening means putting at risk your eternal joy. Nothing really happens for you eternally without being willing to listen, hear, and then immediately obey.

When any of us begin to heed the siren call of pride, we become less willing to listen and follow. We wrap ourselves tightly in our own will, shutting ourselves out from the heavenly guidance intended to make our journey easier. We are like toddlers having a tantrum with eyes and ears tightly clamped shut and completely missing out on the treat being offered to us. We then read by the lamp of our own conceit, choosing a path we think will make us happier. As we walk our own path, we might, like Cain, exclaim, "Now I am free!" (Moses 5:33), buying into the Great Lie that disobedience frees us of having to follow constricting rules and will bring us greater happiness.

Hearkening means being willing to humbly change your present course in the light of inspired new information. It is a willingness to abandon our cherished plans, regardless of how much we might have desired them, in favor of God's divine course for you. It means following the counsel of the still, small voice as completely as you might have responded to a shouted command.

One of the most dramatic examples of this is the Lord's breathtaking command He gave to Abraham to sacrifice Isaac. On the surface, this improbable test seems either 1) grossly unfair, or 2) very confusing, given that the intended sacrifice is the long sought after birthright son.

In addition, this test would almost seem unnecessary given that the Lord had already revealed to Abraham "all the works which my hands have made" as well as all "the intelligences that were organized before the world was." He had already explained, to Abraham's great comfort, this knowledge: "Abraham, thou art one of them; thou wast chosen before thou wast born" (Abraham 3:23).

Thus, if God completely knew Abraham before this life, knew what he was capable of, and had already chosen him because of his premortal faithfulness, why require such a heart-rending test of faith? Why require such a painful trial of one already foreordained and tested? Why ask Abraham to hearken to this command, when he had proved, over and over, his willingness to obey?

The answer is this: there was specific knowledge that Abraham—and Sarah—would only come to know by hearkening to a difficult, almost impossible, assignment. President Spencer W. Kimball explains,

> Father Abraham and Mother Sarah knew—knew the promise would be fulfilled. How? They did not know and did not demand to know. Isaac positively would live to be the father of a numerous posterity. They knew he would, even though he might need to die. They knew he could still be raised from the dead to fulfill the promise, and faith here preceded the miracle.[1]

As covenant parents to a numerous posterity, Abraham and Sarah grew their faith in Heavenly Father through this painful experience. By hearkening, they would also know a little of what Heavenly Father would feel one day in Golgotha. They also gained a greater appreciation for their son, Isaac, who would hearken to the words of his father and give himself up to be placed on the alter of sacrifice. By doing so, they would better understand that another Son would submit to His father's will and drink the bitter cup on a day when there would be no ram in the thicket.

For Abraham and Sarah and Isaac, hearkening also meant gaining precious faith-filling knowledge and testimony. That experience increased their trust in their own obedience. Their confidence in themselves would be strengthened as they saw themselves hearken. This knowledge would give them the power necessary to prepare their children for all the blessings promised to Abraham, Isaac, and Jacob. For them, this specific—horrific—hearkening helped them move ever closer to their salvation.

If this was true of Abraham and Sarah, what about you?

Why does it seem that when I hearken I also have to sacrifice something I really want?

In a nutshell, we struggle to follow whispers because they so often involve sacrifice. Whether you are following a whisper or asking someone to follow your inspired whispering, pride and plans are placed on the altar. Inspiration is likely to run contrary to near-sighted natural man planning. Giving up what we think we want can be difficult.

In truth though, sometimes we end up sacrificing something that is good for something that is better. A friend describes a time when he and his new bride served weekly in the temple. They loved being there and felt blessed by their service. After about a year they became pregnant, and soon his wife needed to be released from her temple assignment. His work increased, and he too was soon released.

Shortly afterward they met the temple president and expressed to him how much they missed their weekly temple service. His reply to them was instructive. "Starting your family was the right thing to do. You are sacrificing your time in the temple, at this point in your life, to do something even more important, becoming parents. At this moment, you might only be able to come to the temple every few months. And that would be just fine."

Sacrificing your will is made much easier when you know the one asking loves you and has your best interest at heart. Feeling loved enables you to trust that the result of your obedience will be worth it. You trust that your sacrifice will have meaning and purpose. Sacrifice, under those circumstances, almost ceases to be a sacrifice.

Think back, for a moment, to Abraham and Isaac as they

approach Mount Moriah. Isaac is carrying the wood for the altar (symbolic of Christ carrying His cross). It soon becomes obvious to Isaac that there is no other sacrifice available other than him. His father is old and could easily be resisted. The only way Isaac will become the offering is if he willingly climbs on the altar and submits.

But Isaac knows that his father loves him. He has been repeatedly taught that he is the covenant, birthright son—the child of the miracle birth and Abraham's promised heir to the covenant. Like Abraham, he may not know why this dilemma is being required of them, but he does know that his father loves him dearly. He also knows that Abraham is obedient to the Lord and that God loves them both. It is for these reasons he willingly submits and exercises his faith. This test is as much a test for Isaac as it is for Abraham. Would he hearken and obey? His willingness to surrender says a great deal about Isaac and his father's love for him.

Whispering, done in gentleness, shaped by love, is effective because it fills others with trust. Sisters, you are called to whisper because you are endowed, as a daughter of Mother Eve, with the God-given gift of nurturing. By its very nature, motherly nurturing was meant to be the loving act that guides the children of men beyond their mortal tendencies of pride and selfishness.

You are the still, small voice a child hears in the middle of the night, a voice filled with calm and love and reassurance. It is your gentle encouragement that lifts a discouraged husband, urging him to try again.

It's also the voice of hysterical screaming when my children are out of their bed for the hundredth time and refuse to go to sleep! It's not so still and small at that point!

True. There is no way you will ever fill this role perfectly. You act, you repent, and you try again the next day. To misquote the prophet Moroni, "And if [mothers have children] I will show unto them their weakness. I give unto [mothers children] that they may be humble; and my grace is sufficient for all [moms] that humble themselves before me" (Ether 12:27).

As you listen and hearken, you will know what to say and when to say it. You will be humbled enough to know that you do not have all the answers and that you need help in your nurturing whispers.

The Tongue of Angels

I take a great amount of comfort from the words of Nephi. He promises that those who are baptized and receive the gift of the Holy Ghost will now be able to "speak with a new tongue, yea, even with the tongue of angels" (2 Nephi 31:14).

We are too quick to relegate the gift of tongues to missionaries learning foreign languages. It is certainly true that so many do receive a gift of tongues so that they can teach the gospel in a native tongue. It is a great gift. However, the gift of tongues also has a much wider application.

Nephi is promising all who are converted and baptized the ability to speak with a new tongue. If we are to speak with the tongue of angels, we will be speaking the words they would say, exactly how they would say it.

Recently I was assigned to speak in church. The youth speaker, very nervous, spoke for about thirty seconds and quickly sat down. There was no other speaker besides than me. Faced with the entire time to fill, I stood up and began. As I started to speak, I prayed for help and inspiration. The words began to flow and ideas flew to my mind. Some of the things I spoke about were unique even to me. I was learning new principles in the very moment I was teaching them.

Very soon I looked up to see that the time was past. I quickly finished and sat down. I knew that the Spirit had taken over. In that moment, I knew that I had been teaching and speaking with a new tongue. Not mine, but the tongue of angels.

The remarkable thing about my experience is that it is not that remarkable. In all probability, you have had a similar experience. You have been teaching a class or speaking in church. You have tried to explain a gospel principle to a child or an investigator to the Church. You have felt the Spirit take over and lift your speech above yourself. You have spoken with words that were not your own. *You have spoken with the tongue of angels!*

Nurturing and whisperings are filled with the voices and words of angels. Whether this inspired intervention is the result of actual angels or the simple flowing of the Spirit really doesn't matter. Your nurturing words will be shaped beyond your own ability.

Notes

1 Spencer W. Kimball, *Faith Precedes the Miracle* (Salt Lake City: Deseret Book, 1972), 1.

10

THE DEWS OF HEAVEN AND THE MARRIAGE DANCE

A distraught wife sat angry and restless in my office. She had a long list of shortcomings she had compiled on her husband. She tearfully described how he was thoughtless, disengaged, short with the kids, a horrible home teacher, and emotionally unavailable most of the time. She tried to talk to him, at my urging, but complained that he didn't respond much and had changed even less. She was frustrated and was trying to decide if she could afford to leave him.

Acting on a sudden thought, I asked, "When did you talk to him?"

"Well," she said, "it was 3:00 a.m., and he'd been asleep." But then she quickly added, "But it still shouldn't have mattered!"

Ah, I thought, *the Marriage Dance strikes again*!

Each marriage relationship is a complicated and refined set of actions and reactions. The behavior of one calls for a response from the other. Over time, each spouse begins to anticipate what the other will do and say in most situations and plans accordingly. It is the Marriage Dance—that unique style of interplay between husband and wife that is as carefully choreographed as any dance troupe.

In the early stages of a relationship, the budding Marriage Dance is performed in the equivalent of wet cement: actions and reactions are still forming and can be easily adapted and changed. Interaction patterns have not yet hardened and are still pretty pliable. Over time, though, those action/reaction dance steps become more and more hardened and predictable. You begin to anticipate what each of you will do in certain situations because you've seen these reactions over and over. One thing is said or done and it's as if the music begins and each of you starts your assigned dialogues and actions.

You each know what comes next.

The Marriage Dance takes focused effort to change because it becomes so ingrained into daily behavior. You say and do things on pure reaction, following the established dance. You might find, for instance, that critical responses leap right out of your mouth as if they had a mind of their own. You say and do things you later regret and have to apologize for. Rather than promoting a respectful relationship, you end up being "acted upon" (2 Nephi 2:14), or reacting and regretting.

The frustrated wife in my office had developed a pattern—a dance pattern—of letting things build up inside until she "blew up." Unfortunately, she often chose times to talk about them when her husband was tired or in the middle of a project and generally late at night when neither of them were at their best. In looking at the problem, she could clearly see that nothing positive was going to happen in those discussions, under those circumstances. It didn't matter how valid her frustrations were, they weren't going to be heard and she'd be left even more angry than before.

Her new plan called for finding moments when both of them

could focus on critical issues without being interrupted. She also chose times when she was feeling calm and ready to speak in quieter tones. In return, she found her husband less defensive and more open to hearing her concerns. Slowly, she began to change the Marriage Dance.

At this point, you've been reading a lot of what husband whispering is supposed to look and feel like. Instinctively, you've compared it to your own relationship pattern. Rather than becoming too discouraged—look first at your own marriage or relationship dance and ask yourself some simple questions:

Can I clearly describe our marriage dance? That is, can I identify each action and the reaction in our dance? Is there a predictable pattern of when I do this, he does this, then I say this, and he then says or does something like this?

Which part of your dance causes the most pain? Is there an aspect of the action/reaction cycle that results in the most painful responses on your part—the one that most makes whispering difficult? Are there things that are routinely said that continue to ring in your ears?

How often do you react and respond out of anger rather than speaking from the more tender (and deeper feelings) of hurt and fear? When you react out of feelings of anger, you say things designed to push others away. *Anger is fueled by a need to protect yourself.* You emotionally defend your sense of "what's fair" or attempt to even the score. On the other hand, when you remove the anger and quietly explain how something said or done hurt your feelings, you open the door for more honest discussions.

Can you visualize how softer answers might lead toward a different, more effective dance?

One of hallmarks of cowboy horse whisperers is their patience. They purposefully keep moving forward with their teaching but are patient in allowing the young horses to be comfortable with new behaviors over time. As the young horses feel safety and gentle confidence from their trainers, they become less reactive. They respond more easily and consistently.

In a similar way, husband whispering was never meant to be a quick fix. It is learning to communicate heaven's way, with love and patience. It is allowing needed time for destructive marriage dance styles to modify and change. The Savior's explanation that we need to forgive "seventy times seven" simply means "keep doing it as long as it takes!"

The Lord taught Joseph Smith many important lessons about how to deal with difficult people. Imprisoned in Liberty Jail, he thought a great deal about those who'd been in leadership positions in the Church and how differently those leaders had responded, positively and negatively, during the stresses of the Missouri mobbings. Part of what Joseph was taught is described in Section 121 of the Doctrine and Covenants as we've discussed in an earlier chapter.

The key to changing a destructive marriage dance comes from verse 45. "The doctrine of the priesthood," the Lord explains, "shall distill upon thy soul as the dews from heaven."

That style of learning is pretty enlightening. On a cool morning, if I chose, I could sit outside my own house and wait for the morning dew to show up. If I did, I would never see it arrive. I wouldn't observe a deluge of dew or a downpour of dew. I would never get to watch a dew drizzle. This is because dew distills. It quietly forms amid the quiet of the morning without fanfare. The moisture condenses out of the air and slowly appears. Without warning, it is just there.

Interesting that the Lord uses this particular analogy to teach us about how we learn critical doctrines of the priesthood. No deluges or downpours or drizzles. A quiet distilling. We are to learn, drop by drop, line upon line, without any fanfare. We learn as we listen to whispering and soon discover we know more than we thought we did. If we stay on the right path, that knowledge continues to grow within us until it comes to a perfect brightness.

In a similar way, angry behavior and destructive habits are best altered by dew-like soft conversations. They form the foundation of a more loving marriage dance, one that can heal and support and build powerful bonds. They set a tone where important matters are discussed and resolved. They help form an atmosphere of respect.

In their calling as nurturer, women, wives, and mothers are uniquely endowed with an innate ability to establish this powerful congenial tone. You can teach families what gentleness sounds like. They learn from your example how it sounds and feels. They begin to alter their tone to match yours. In turn, they are being prepared to respond to quiet whispers that come from beyond the veil.

The key element in all of this is patience. You might think that changing the tone in your family is tantamount to making a U-turn in an aircraft carrier. And you'd be right! Contentiousness in a family has a lot of built-in momentum. *I get mad because you got mad at me. You said things so I said things. You raised your voice and so I had to raise mine to be heard. What you did wasn't really fair, so why should I be fair?*

Reversing all of that is not quick or easy. It requires consistency in your determination to create a gentler interaction between each of you. It means being patient when patient is the last thing you want to do!

Recently I watched this kind of effective patience in action. I was sitting in an airport during an approaching snowstorm. The weather channel was forecasting a dire, life-changing snowstorm of the century and people were frantically trying to get on a plane before a snowy apocalypse descended.

One particular businessman forcefully approached an airline employee at the gate. The man was obviously used to getting his way, and the snowstorm was destroying his well-made plans. He began demanding—loudly—that special arrangements be made just for him. And he wasn't about to take no for an answer. There was no question what he wanted because anyone in a ten-mile radius of the airport would have heard him.

He yelled, he belittled, he threatened, and he even pointed. He was a force of nature all by himself. What was most impressive to me, however, was the airline employee. She was in an impossible position and she could do little under the snowy circumstances. What she did was handle Mr. Redface with a quiet professionalism that was impressive to watch and was a model for every mom who has ever had a teenage child.

Her response to every verbal blast began with a soft, "I understand, sir. But I'm unable to do that." And then she would explain why. He would yell again and she would repeat, "I understand, sir." This happened over and over. She never raised her voice but never did she vary from what she could do and could not do. She was gentle but firm and fixed. As I watched, the angry customer slowly began to match her voice and tone. He was still demanding. But he now was noticeably quieter and beginning to speak in a more problem-solving tone of voice. Her consistent approach changed him completely and helped move things toward a resolution.

Whispering can stand as a certain calm in the storm, an example of a much saner life. But never is whispering weaker or more vulnerable. Whispering stands confident amid what is right and does not waver under pressure.

Trusting in the power of whispering does not happen right away. Neither do husbands and family immediately trust it. It is only believed as it softens family dialogue and leaves a more genial spirit.

The Magic Sock Drawer

Years ago, Cindy and I had read of a couple whose marriage was deeply in trouble. Each had become expert in pointing out the flaws in the other. They were particularly good at seizing the moment and quickly announcing each irritating imperfection. Like a painful tennis match, each day was a constant game of back and forth, studiously making sure the other knew just how much misery they brought on the other.

Then, in a fit of wild desperation, the husband unfairly and unexpectedly changed tactics. One morning, as he reached into his drawer, he commented, "Hey, I think I have a magic sock drawer! Each week my socks magically appear in my drawer, clean and folded. It's as if they just magically appear out of nowhere. Thank you!"

The wife was quickly thrown off track by this grossly unfair change in the game. She silently nodded back to him, trying vainly to understand just how this comment would eventually turn around into another scathing attack. To her surprise, her cunning husband simply finished getting ready and left for work without saying anything else about drawers or socks.

Nothing!

And, of course, his comment worked really well. She was miserable the rest of the day, trying to decipher his comment. She spent hours trying to analyze what his next devious move would be. She finally decided he had carefully set her up with a seeming compliment just so he could level her later on with an attack. She spent all day gearing up for the second phase of his new plan, strategizing on how to reply to him when it occurred.

The second stage of his plan for her misery unfolded later that night. At a moment when her guard was down, he swooped in for the next blow.

"I noticed," he stated innocently, "that the dishes in the dishwasher magically seem to have made it to the cupboard. Thank you for doing that."

And that was all he said.

Now she was totally lost. His comment was so shrewd and so devious that he'd even delivered it with a complete straight face. To make it worse, he'd even *looked* sincere. And there was no follow-up comment. Which, by the way, would have been completely effective given that her jaw was firmly on the floor, even after she'd silently nodded an obligatory thank-you.

What is he up to? she wondered.

Later that night, she lay awake still trying to see where all this was going. Somewhere around 3:00 a.m., the beginnings of a counterattack started to form in her brain. The more she thought of it, the more she could see how her new plan was her only real defense. His devilish attack needed—no, demanded—a similar blow in return.

She carefully chose her moment the next morning. Just as he was preparing to leave, she looked carefully at him. After a deep breath, she repeated the line she'd practiced all night, "I noticed just how hard you're working. Thank you!"

She was silently gratified when she saw the look of shock streak across his face. He just stared blankly at her, bracing for the coming caustic statement. But, sticking firmly to her plan, she just innocently stared back. After a moment, he mumbled an awkward thank-you and hurried out the door. She watched as he walked to the car and glanced several times over his shoulder at the house, his face still a look of confusion and loss.

"Bingo!" She grinned. "Hit the bull's-eye!"

The rest of her day was actually quite pleasant. Where the day before she'd been worried and frustrated, today she was totally at peace. She knew that if he'd chosen to play dirty like that, she could reply in kind. He'd upped his game—but so had she. She confidently went about her day, ready for whatever comment he might want to throw at her later.

And he did! He continued to make odd but positive comments about her cooking, the bills she paid, even her appearance. And rather than let those comments get her down, she fired back compliments about some things he fixed around the house and the fact that he'd taken her car to be washed.

As you might imagine, after the initial confusion, both became less miserable and their comments were said more sincerely. The mood in the house soon changed dramatically. They smiled more and attacked each other less.

And it all began with a comment about the magic sock drawer.

The emotional temperature of a home determines a great deal about the lessons that can be taught and how those around you will respond to them. You work to whisper change even though you chide yourself for sometimes being the problem. The role of whisperer and nurturer does not go to the perfect, only the willing.

So much of your life is affected by the tone of your relationships. It helps determine how you feel about yourself, how your husband and kids see themselves. Loving conversations help prepare your heart to hear and respond to loving responses from heaven. The peace you feel from heaven will then help you better modify what you say and do as you interact with others around you.

The Temple

Finally, you will learn great lessons about whispering from regular temple attendance. In the Old Testament, Father Jacob is awakened in the night to a great vision of the "ladder set up on the earth and the top of it reached to heaven." As he visited with the Lord, Jacob learned much of what the Lord had in store for him and his posterity to come.

When he awoke, Jacob exclaimed, "Surely the Lord is in this place." In response, he named the place Beth-el, meaning the House of God, and placed a stone pillar there as a memorial of his experience. He also made a vow before the pillar, promising that "the Lord be my God" (Genesis 28).

In the Book of Revelation, the Apostle John seems to refer to this incident when he quotes the Lord, saying, "Behold, I come quickly: hold that fast which thou hast, that no man take thy crown. *Him that overcometh will I make a pillar in the temple of my God . . .* and I will write upon him the name of my God" (Revelation 3:11–12; emphasis added).

In other words, those that worship in the temple become pillars—memorials—of God and His goodness. They carry His name and "stand as a witnesses of God at all times and in all things, and in all places" (Mosiah 18:9) of what He has done for the children of men.

You carry His name. You stand as a pillar. As such, your speech and behaviors will be softened as the dews from heaven until, finally, you will allow him to become "the speaker of all your words and the doer of all your deeds."

CONCLUSION

Years ago, horses trainers came to understand an important principle: horses respond better to soft gentle directions. True, they might react to yelling or harsh techniques, but the result was a dispirited horse, broken in spirit as well as behavior.

A careful reading of the scriptures reveals that Heavenly Father first chooses to interact with His children in the same way. Speaking in a still, small voice helps preserve our agency and our willingness to chose. That voice is not weaker, rather it "maketh my bones to quake"(D&C 85:6). His voice reaches down into our soul and fills us with His light and knowledge. It removes the darkness of the world, helping us to better see our path back to Him.

Whispering is heaven's way of communicating. It is God's pattern for us, an example of how He intends for us to interact with each other. This is especially true when it comes to husbands and wives. As a woman, your very nature, your spiritual stewardship as a daughter of Mother Eve, is deeply rooted in nurturing. It is this transforming power that shapes and forms the children of men everywhere. In its gentleness lies its very strength.

Unfortunately, some will misunderstand the purpose of whispering. For instance, they might read some of this book and think I am recommending the gentle art of womanly manipulation. Or they might think what is being suggested here is a way to get what you want through feigned weakness or phony submissiveness.

Nothing could be further from the truth. Whispering is not a series of communication techniques to master, dragging them out when nothing else is working. Whispering, in general, and husband whispering, specifically, is the foreordained way to communicate truth in a firm but loving way. Spoken in loving tones, you provide nurturing counsel and support, as dictated by the deep love you feel. Contrast that with the times you speak out of frustration, anger, or fear and you quickly see the difference.

Gentle touch and softer tones combine with firm eye contact to communicate powerfully those things that need to be said. Husbands will respond differently because you are approaching them differently. When heart is speaking to heart, your full intent is better heard. His defensiveness is reduced and opposition begins to decrease.

A word of warning! If your marriage dance has been contentious in nature, your first few attempts at whispering will seem as if your words are lost in the wind. For instance, if you have kids, you might have trained them that only when you yell are you serious. They might hear you tell them to clean up their room the first ten times you ask them, but only when you raise your voice are you now "serious." Their internal clock tells them to wait for the eleventh time, combined with yelling, before they face any real consequences.

Husbands are much the same way. We know that a certain tone of voice or level of irritation says that you are now *really* serious. Anything short of that and we might not have to respond yet.

For this reason, husband whispering might be a major change in your marriage dance. If it is, you will need to allow time for him to learn the new dance steps. A soft voice can also be a firm voice in expressing your concerns and your needs. But it might need to be repeated more at first. Remember, you might be changing the rules here! Husbands—and kids—will be watching to see if you are truly changing or if this is a short-term approach that will be soon abandoned if it does not work.

Good luck!

ABOUT THE AUTHOR

Returning author Kevin Hinckley is a licensed professional counselor in private practice. He received his master's degree in counseling from Brigham Young University with an emphasis in organizational behavior. He has developed numerous therapeutic programs, including inpatient and day treatment programs for addiction and trauma recovery. He has worked closely with the LDS Addiction Recovery Program and is the creator of The Naaman Project, a day treatment program for pornography addiction. A former bishop and institute teacher, Kevin has written four other books: *Habits, Hurts & Hangups*, *Promptings or Me?*, *Parenting the Strong-Willed Child*, and *Burying Our Swords*. He is a regular presenter at Campus Education Weeks at BYU–Idaho and BYU.